Denuded Devotion to Christ

Princeton Theological Monograph Series

K. C. Hanson, Charles M. Collier, D. Christopher Spinks,
Robin Parry, and Rodney Clapp, Series Editors

Recent volumes in the series:

Atsuyoshi Fujiwara
*Theology of Culture in a Japanese Context:
A Believers' Church Perspective*

Koo Dong Yun
*The Holy Spirit and Ch'i (Qi):
A Chiological Approach to Pneumatology*

Stanley S. MacLean
*Resurrection, Apocalypse, and the Kingdom of Christ:
The Eschatology of Thomas F. Torrance*

Brian Neil Peterson
*Ezekiel in Context: Ezekiel's Message Understood in Its Historical
Setting of Covenant Curses and Ancient Near Eastern
Mythological Motifs*

Amy E. Richter
Enoch and the Gospel of Matthew

Maeve Louise Heaney
Music as Theology: What Music Says about the Word

Eric M. Vail
Creation and Chaos Talk: Charting a Way Forward

David L. Reinhart
*Prayer as Memory: Toward the Comparative Study of Prayer
as Apocalyptic Language and Thought*

Denuded Devotion to Christ

The Ascetic Piety of Protestant True Religion in the Reformation

LARRY D. HARWOOD

With a Foreword by William L. Isley Jr.

☙PICKWICK *Publications* · Eugene, Oregon

DENUDED DEVOTION TO CHRIST
The Ascetic Piety of Protestant True Religion in the Reformation

Princeton Theological Monograph Series 191

Copyright © 2012 Larry D. Harwood. All rights reserved. Except for brief quotations in critical publications or reviews, no part of this book may be reproduced in any manner without prior written permission from the publisher. Write: Permissions, Wipf and Stock Publishers, 199 W. 8th Ave., Suite 3, Eugene, OR 97401.

Pickwick Publications
An Imprint of Wipf and Stock Publishers
199 W. 8th Ave., Suite 3
Eugene, OR 97401

www.wipfandstock.com

ISBN 13: 978-1-61097-076-1

Cataloguing-in-Publication data:

Harwood, Larry D.

    Denuded Devotion to Christ : The Ascetic Piety of Protestant True Religion in the Reformation / Larry D. Harwood ; with a foreword by William L. Isley Jr.

    xxiv + 146 pp. ; 23 cm. Includes bibliographical references.

    Princeton Theological Monograph Series 191

    ISBN 13: 978-1-61097-076-1

    1. Pietism—History. 2. Reformation. 3. Karlstadt, Andreas Rudolff-Bodenstein von, ca. 1480–1541. 4. Zwingli, Ulrich, 1484–1531. 5. Calvin, Jean, 1509–1564. I. Isley, William L., Jr. II. Title. III. Series.

BR307 H37 2012

Manufactured in the U.S.A.

I dedicate this work to my beloved wife Dottie. The subject of this book first surfaced between us over a quarter century ago, and we have discussed the ideas within these pages almost endlessly. Were it not for her and her encouragement, I might have kept our conversations only conversations without ever conceiving of this book. I wish to thank her for all the patience and fortitude she has shown with reference to both me and this book.

May God richly bless.

No one has seen God at any time;
the Son, who is in the Father, has proclaimed him.

—St. John's Gospel 1:18

Contents

Foreword / ix
Preface / xiii
Acknowledgments / xix
List of Abbreviations / xxi

The Rational Philosophical Consciousness / 1
Karlstadt, Zwingli, and Calvin on True Religion / 29
Protestantism and Rationalism / 58
The Aesthetic in the Practice of True Religion / 83
True Religion and the Philosophical Consciousness / 105
Afterword—True Religion and Puritan Consciousness / 133

Bibliography / 141

Foreword

Denuded Devotion to Christ argues that early Protestantism, especially Reformed Protestantism, in its efforts to combat the perceived errors and abuses of late medieval Christianity by limiting the material aspect of the Christian faith, was characterized by a kind of philosophical rationalism. This is not, however, your ordinary academic book, nor one of merely historical interest. Indeed, it is a quite extraordinary book, combining academic excellence and rigor with an integrative approach utilizing philosophy and theology, both in their analytic and historical strains, to discuss passionately the theme of Christian devotion, in particular the deleterious effect of the mistrust of the material in Reformed piety and worship.

Dr. Harwood is just the man to write such a wide-ranging work of contemporary relevance. Larry, for he is a former colleague and longtime friend, is a professional philosopher whose special interest in aesthetics allows him to bring a fruitful interpretation of Reformed theology that a specialist in the early Reformation, such as I, would have missed. At the same time, he is a committed Christian who thus brings a heartfelt concern for Christian spirituality to his research. It is this happy combination of scholarship and religious dedication that makes *Denuded Devotion to Christ* a particularly important work that deserves a hearing both in the halls of the academy and the sanctuaries of the church.

The essential problem is that the reformers' quest for true religion or pure worship led to the exaltation of the "naked Christ" or what Dr. Harwood calls "naked truth." Naked truth is the notion that matter interferes with theological thought and religious piety. It identifies the spirit with the immaterial and, as Dr. Harwood effectively demonstrates, that means with human mental capacities. Shockingly, and I would add unintentionally, the reformers' passionate concern for *sola gratia* resulted in a piety that left man before God stripped of all his humanity except his mind.

How did this happen? How could it have happened? It seems to me that they failed to grasp, as we all too often do as well, the significance of John's assertion that the Word became flesh and dwelt among us, that truth

Foreword

is found in the Incarnate Son of God. In particular the Swiss reformers, exhibiting the influence of the platonic strains of the humanist reformers, distrusted the material. For Christian theologians, both Calvin and Zwingli spoke too disparagingly of the body and so, contrary to their desire, linked themselves with what Dr. Harwood calls "the god of the philosophers." In Zwingli's case it would appear to have left the body of Jesus with the merely functional role of being something to sacrifice.

As with all insightful scholarship, Dr. Harwood's achievement raises many questions and opens up several fruitful avenues of research which I hope scholars will follow up on. Let me just point briefly to a few in the areas of historical research, epistemology and theological anthropology and the nature of reformation.

Incredible as it may seem, with regard to historical research, there is much that still needs to be done in this already heavily investigated era. What, if any, was the relationship between Karlstadt and the Swiss Reformation? Even more broadly, how does the notion of naked truth show us new ways of looking at the connections between Renaissance humanism, especially that of Erasmus, the Swiss Reformation, and the Anabaptists? Dr. Harwood rightly exempts Luther from the temptation to bow before the god of the philosophers, but what of Melanchthon? Calvin and he, both more influenced by humanism, carried on a friendly correspondence concerning the sacrament of communion and appeared to be closer in their views than Luther would have liked. What of the Anglicans? The earlier Anglicans, such as Cranmer, were strongly influenced by Reformed Protestantism, but seemed to have largely escaped the dangers of naked truth. Why? And I do not think that it was solely because they were afraid of Henry VIII.

On an even broader scale, Dr. Harwood raises again the question of the relationship between Calvinism and modernity. He develops convincingly a very interesting connection between Calvinism's distrust of the material and Hegel's philosophical consciousness and the movement toward modernity. Could this philosophical tendency be played out in the socio-economic realm in unexpected ways? We should take another look at Max Weber and his school again.

In epistemology, we desperately need to understand how we know as humans. Naked truth runs the risk of seeing us merely as mental calculating machines, but the human mind is not isolated from the human body. We think as whole beings. How do we understand this without falling into the swamp of subjectivity? Surely, Jesus' claim that he is the truth should show us the way out of this dilemma.

The epistemological issues are intimately related to theological anthropology. Naked truth limits the image of God to man's mind or mental capacities because this seems to be the most spiritual and therefore like unto God who is spirit. But does not this smack of the pagan notion of some kind of divine spark in man, something in him that he actually shares with God? The biblical notion of the image of God encompasses the whole person and his actions without allowing in any way for putting the creature on the same ontological level with his Creator.

I believe that Dr. Harwood's thesis demonstrates that reformation is always haunted by the dangers of naked truth. Certainly political ideology that leads to destructive revolutions bears this out when it seeks to tear down all human traditions and institutions and create a perfectly rational society, but religious reformation shows a similar tendency. Without a doubt, human traditions can and do become accretions that cover up and distort the faith. The religious reformer then almost necessarily thinks in terms of stripping all of this away and rediscovering the core or essence of true religion. Somehow we need to avoid the delusion that we create a pure worship by freeing devotion from the human element. The Word became flesh and dwelt among us. He was seen, touched and heard. That is how God wants to be known and worshipped.

Finally, and in all seriousness, I ask, "Do we Protestants need to become Catholics or Orthodox?" I think not. The excesses and abuses that a Calvin and an Erasmus saw were real. They misunderstood those errors and so came up with a distorted solution. How do we understand the errors that they saw and how can we correct them without falling into different ones?

As an evangelical Protestant, I am concerned about the state of the evangelical church. Yes, contemporary worship does seem to want to appeal to the visual senses and involve the body more in worship. At the same time, it gives clear evidence of downplaying the place of the proclamation of the word and often is quite resistant and even hostile to serious theological critique. These are the same problems that Calvin saw in the church of his day.

The academy and, even more, the church should be grateful to Dr. Harwood for this profound study. It should be given serious consideration not only for its specific historical thesis but for its broad implications.

Foreword

Denuded Devotion to Christ raises the question of what it means to be human in the light of gospel's claim that God became man in order to bring men, not disembodied spirits, to himself.

Dr. William L. Isley Jr.
May, 2012
Topeka, Kansas

Preface

THIS BOOK EXAMINES A HISTORICALLY INFLUENTIAL IDEAL OF CHRISTIAN religious practice and surveys Protestant Reformation theologians defending it in their conception of "true religion." I will claim in the pages following that with this ideal, these reformers, however unintentionally, supported a notion of God similar to the "god of the philosophers." Furthermore, in their advocacy of true religion, these reformers implied that the ideal practitioner of true religion should resemble and indeed live like a philosopher, in a sense to be explained in the pages that follow.

I am not making these claims with reference to all Protestants at the time of the Reformation, but to a smaller group, the Reformed tradition, stemming from John Calvin and others. This book, however, is not encouraging abandonment of Reformed Protestantism, nor encouraging becoming Catholic or Lutheran, however much the Reformed thinkers surveyed were in large part critiquing their Catholic and Lutheran theological adversaries. However, it is a book about some particulars of a vaunted religious ideal, and though antedating the Reformation, much Reformation Protestantism beyond the Reformed faction accelerated this ideal into a staple of modern Christian devotion, primarily of course among Protestants, but particularly so among orthodox Protestants. The particulars of this conception of true religion have a seductive simplicity that resonates with much religious practice through the ages, though the ideal provokes too little reflection before assuming too unquestioningly congruence with the Christian religion. Moreover, this ideal—historically fashioned as a reforming principle—permeates many Christian communities of the past and present, and indeed will continue to influence the future.

I write about this phenomenon from within the Reformed theological tradition, simply because it is the Christian tradition I happen to know best. The judgments I make of the Reformed tradition in what follows are not unique to that tradition, for the phenomenon I speak of is easily found in varying degrees in many other Christian traditions, and indeed can be seen in non-Christian religious traditions as well. Moreover, the popularity of this religious ideal advances from roots in a kind of basic or natural religion and thus often makes a timeless appeal to common sense. The ideal is also not infrequently called upon as correction to what are deemed religious excesses violating the form of religion assumed by religious reformers, Christian and otherwise. However, the particulars of this ideal for reform are often only faintly Christian, but strongly rationalistic. This is why I have written the book: particulars of this ideal of true religion dictate many details of Christian religious life and worship, but the ideal is dubiously predisposed for the religion it presumes to bolster.

However, in focusing upon the Reformed tradition as my example, that tradition is not deemed the worst offender of what I critique in the pages that follow. Indeed, the point of this book is not about indicting a particular Christian tradition, but rather critiquing a conception of God and human anthropology shared by diverse Christian traditions dutifully emulating a rational ideal often assumed as Christian in character.

The treatment of a subject which might be termed invasive rationalism, moreover, will invite misinterpretation. That is, while I am an Anglican adherent of the Reformed theological tradition, I am also by training and trade a Christian philosopher, and therefore, one interpretation of this work might wrongly mistake the philosopher author as finally understanding correctly the incoherence of Athens and reason when applied to Jerusalem or Christian beliefs. However, I am not following, for example, the route of the medieval Islamic thinker Al-Ghazali, as I understand him. Al-Ghazali began to charge the philosophers of his day with heresy as regarded the faith, while himself having recourse to the mystical theologies of his Islamic tradition. My direction in this book, in a general way, is something of the reverse. That is, I am contending that the theologians of my study advance a questionable form of religious devotion in much of their critique of the material and tangible practices of sacramental religion. These theologians, therefore, I see as relying upon too much rationalism in the defense of their notion of proper religious devotion. I am of course not impugning these theologians for an idea, much less for an idea because it shares historical kinship to a philosophical ideal, but rather for advancing dubious particulars when applied to the Christian religion. Therefore, in this work, neither do I impugn philosophy as philosophy or reason as reason with my claim that a kind of spiritualizing rationalism intrudes upon the worship of the Christian God in this idealized conception. Rather, in evaluating a portion of the Reformation history of striving to live out and practice true religion,

I maintain that an adequate conception of the Christian God bears only remote likeness to the god of the philosophers, and that worshippers of the Christian God need not be reborn as models of cognitive and philosophical creatures who set no store by the material world and its resonances and rhythms in their religious conceptions and practices. In this work, I will refer to these critiqued conceptions and to the anthropological commitments of this ideal as exhibiting allegiance toward a kind of "naked truth." Said another way, there is a denuded devotion to the Christian God by human worshippers, neither of whom exist in the form of the devotional model encouraged in the critiqued conception of "true religion."

Nor do I fault the theologians discussed in these pages as owning all responsibility for the popularity of their judgments about the practice of true religion. This is because these conceptions are not the province of intellectuals only, or even theologians or philosophers in particular. The briefest foray into the history of the Christian Church reveals among many lay Christians sympathy for a God conceptualized like the philosopher's god, with encouragement given to an attendant human anthropology appropriate to the worship of such a god.

What I argue in this work is perhaps beneficially contrasted to the work of other philosophers of rightful note in the Reformed tradition, for much current philosophical interest in the Protestant Reformed religious tradition centers on "Reformed epistemology" as articulated and defended by Alvin Plantinga, Nicholas Wolterstorff, and George Mavrodes, among others. In Reformed epistemology as characterized by these philosophers, Christian religious belief is categorized, in Plantinga's words, as "epistemologically basic." This position is acknowledged to be derived from the thought of John Calvin, the sixteenth century Protestant reformer.

Such a position may create the impression that the Reformed tradition is free of the rationalizing temptation provoking the religious believer to produce an account or justification of that belief amenable to rational demands.

My argument in this book, however, is that the impression of independence from rational containment is only partially the case in this tradition, because a proclivity to rationalism *is* strong and evident in the early Reformed thinkers of the Protestant Reformation. Indeed, this feature of Reformed devotion and worship has long been noted by scholars describing this tradition, while rarely touched upon by most within the tradition. The resonances between the Reformed tradition and a kind of philosophical rationalism, while not reflecting common aims at the level of ideology (or theology), nonetheless reflect some common epistemological, anthropological, and metaphysical commitments that are evident in comparing the rationalism prominent in portions of the historical Western tradition of philosophy to these early Reformed religious thinkers. Thus, though not seeking to advance philosophically at the time of the early Reformation, but instead to arrive at what this tradition called true religion, the Reformed tradition nevertheless weakens Christian consciousness with a devotional rationalism in that quest for true religion.

The Reformed tradition of course shares in the general Protestant opposition to philosophy characteristic of the early Reformation. However, in Luther, opposition to philosophy becomes most strenuous at the very level where it remains in force in the Reformed tradition. The reticence of Luther toward philosophy is basically over its rationalism. In the Reformed tradition, its own rationalism is responsible for what sympathy it has with philosophy. Contrary to the common and understandable perception of Protestants and philosophers as pursing disparate routes to truth, as in, for example, reliance upon revelation or reason respectively, I argue that in this early Reformed tradition, there is a latent rationalism vying to progressively elevate religious communion between God and the worshipper to levels proportionately distant from the senses and material media. In the transformation of religious practice by these Reformed thinkers, their negative critique of the association of materiality to religion takes the form of the charges of ritualism, superstition, and idolatry. Meanwhile, the religious ideal of these reformers insists that the devotional life of true religion be lived largely bereft of materiality because of these attendant liabilities.

Many of the material aspects of religion in this conception seem foreign and therefore are frequently minimized or sacrificed in this notion of true religion. This disunion comes about because a Reformed Protestantism that sought a reformation of aids to worship incorporated rationalism as a Protestant principle by a strenuous and halting preference for the spiritual over the sensual. In the most zealous Reformed combating of possible occasion for idolatry, the antipathy toward the sensual and material elements of religious devotion pushed some early Reformed thinkers toward a conception of religious truth and practice increasingly bereft of material elements. There is, therefore, a corresponding restraint placed upon the human soul to find virtually all spiritual nourishment in a spiritual God, and largely without the means of material aids. In this conception, because the Christian aids to devotion to God are teeming with the potential of idolatry, much of the piety of the early Reformed tradition, in the desire to draw closer to the divine, as a consequence, paradoxically draws closer to rationalism in how God is conceptualized—and to the metaphysical mind-god of rationalism and implicitly to the god of the philosophers. Accordingly, the devotee of God assumes the psychological or mental pose of a philosopher.

The affinity of the Reformed thinkers for the rationalism characteristic of philosophy is not for the most part an affinity for philosophy. Rather, it is an affinity for rationalism, which accounts for the peculiar and paradoxical affinity of these Protestants for the rational mind of the philosopher, with *anthropos philosophicus* esteemed as the truest human model for the practice of true religion. It is scarcely cause for wonder, then, that many scholars have seen in the particulars of this expression of true religion the unintended cultivation of later modern rationalism. For that reason, my first chapter will briefly engage this legacy of the Reformed tradition.

In philosophical terms, the reticence of the Reformed tradition toward the religious value of materiality is a transformation from a religious to a rational philosophical consciousness. The nineteenth century Protestant German philosopher Hegel offers justifications for such an historical change, and in this work, I will take some issue with Hegel's positive estimation of such an historical transition, while I nevertheless make use of his conceptual terminology. Moreover, my inquiry concerns the attitude toward materiality by the early Reformed thinkers that accomplishes this feat in terms of a transformation of religious consciousness. I will claim that in slighting or dismissing material considerations from Christian devotion, sectors of Protestantism moved true religion into a philosophical consciousness as evidenced by the practices of true religion.

In making the claims of this book, I am not contending merely for the logical truism that any religion or ideology in its assertions embraces some philosophy or philosophical form, no matter how emphatic its denial of such. Rather, and contrary to Hegel, I argue that the negative judgment upon the propriety of material components and resonances for religious devotion represents something of a depleting historical shift of consciousness in Christian practice and devotion to the Christian God.

At the same time, this transformed religious culture provided a needed reformation of how the Christian religious world comported with the secular world, and indeed, in some particulars, rightly disciplined medieval

Preface

models of Christian religious devotion run amuck. Nevertheless, my larger estimation is that the change of religious consciousness often expresses itself as a kind of religion scarcely congruent with the material facets of the Christian religion. Moreover, the shift from a robust, though admittedly at times excessive, material Christian practice toward a stage of trimmed religious worship may end by impugning virtually anything for religious devotion except the human mind in communion with the mind of God. Meanwhile, many of the aids to Christian devotion are averted and castigated so as to ensure having only God. This religious ideal, however, revolves around a notion of truth as "naked"—as sufficient because it is true, but nevertheless foundering in lacking a robust conception of the material dimensions of Christian truth, while the conception promoted is significantly indebted to a rational and spiritualizing point of view. This particular, but still popular, ideal of true religion truncates Christian consciousness, life, and devotion, as it nevertheless, in part ushered in the modern Western world.

Acknowledgments

THIS BOOK HAS BENEFITED FROM THE SUGGESTIONS, ENCOURAGEMENT, and evaluations of many people at various stages of writing. The book began with the first thoughts I jotted down after conversations with innumerable people, but principally, my wife Dottie, to whom I owe the greatest thanks for our talks over the years—and still now—on this topic. To my longtime friend Dr. William L. Isley Jr., I owe an incalculable debt for provocative discussions from years past on this subject and for his kind consent to write a foreword for the book. It is sincerely appreciated. To his wife Mary, I extend my thanks for allowing my wife and me so much time with them in Portugal many years ago; our pleasant memories of that time never cease. To my son Theodore and my daughter Elspeth, I am infinitely grateful for both of them allowing their dad to steal away to work on this book at various and inconvenient times, most often when we could have been watching Brewers' or Packers' games together.

I wish to thank with sincere gratitude my Dean, Dr. Glena Temple, for her unwavering and constant support for this piece of writing. Most writers know how often one must fight to keep the pen going for a book to be the result. Knowing that I had her unflagging support kept me moving, however slowly, through the periods of drought and distraction. To my department head, Dr. Bill Reese, I owe hearty thanks for his patience and infinite kindness to a department member whose projects and geographical destinations were not always predictable. I wish to extend warm thanks to Rev. Dr. Tom Duncan, who very kindly took the time to read the entire manuscript and made many helpful criticisms that have found their way into the text. To Judy Ulland, I will be forever grateful for the careful attention she first gave to reading a single chapter of the work, and afterward, for expending a considerable amount of time to do a meticulous reading of the entire manuscript. She was extraordinarily gracious to me to take on this amount of work, and I shall not forget her undaunted willingness to do it. To Lindsay Cummings, Naomi Stennes-Spidahl, and Emily Ackerman, I extend enormous and heartfelt thanks for reading individual chapters of

Acknowledgments

the manuscript and suggesting many helpful corrections in the text. I shall not forget warnings from all my readers about the long sentences of philosophers that may provoke a reader to gasp or go away. To Tsz Wai Tsang, I wish to express thanks for her extensive help on formatting the text more than once, and I wish her all the best on her return to Hong Kong.

To the reader who undertakes to read this book, it will be apparent that I have selectively chosen only a very small portion of material to discuss a topic that could be pursued from a variety of directions and disciplines. The path that I have chosen is therefore a limited one and maybe and probably not the best one. However, the enormity of the subject and its allied topics—and especially the limitations of my own expertise and competence—constrained me in the direction and with the narrowed discipline focus that readers will encounter in these pages.

Though many scholars have written about this topic in different ways, many more are the people having the experience written about in these pages. As one of those people, my analysis aims to present the topic from the standpoint of those in the sanctuary of the church, but in addition, from a scholar's study, with an insistence on trying to understand the phenomenon both philosophically and historically. Therefore, I have tried to write the book for the lay person and not just or even for the scholar. To write a unified work, however, while desirous of appealing to two different audiences, is almost necessarily to aspire for the impossible. For this reason, at times some protracted discussions may tax the patience of readers wanting to see the subject engaged always on the floor and not from the balcony. Perhaps I can excuse myself partly by requiring Hegel to share some of the responsibility for this and with good reason, for it was from reading Hegel that I first conjured up the idea of using his distinction between the religious and philosophical consciousness to focus the large and unwieldy topic found within these few pages. Lastly, to the scholar who is not a Christian believer, but is nevertheless interested in this topic and my exposition of the issues, I bid that reader consider the eternal riches that can be had at the foot of the Cross of Christ who came into the world as one of us for us.

To God be the glory.

Abbreviations

Calvin

References to Calvin's work are from the Corpus Reformatorum edition, *Ioannis Calvini Opera quae supersunt omnia*, Volumes 29–87, eds. Wilhelm Baum, Eduard Cunitz and Eduard Reuss (Brunswick and Berlin, 1863–1900). My citations from Calvin refer to the volume number and pagination of the Corpus Reformatorum, shortened to CR. In addition, I include the name of the individual work within the CR, and also a reference to the English translations of Calvin by Henry Beveridge, *The Institutes of the Christian Religion* (Grand Rapids: Eerdmans, 1975), and Henry Beveridge, *Tracts and Treatises in Defense of the Reformed Faith*, 3 volumes (Grand Rapids: Eerdmans, 1958), to accommodate both scholarly and lay readers. Thus, in citations from Calvin, my first listed reference is from the Corpus Reformatorum edition, followed by the reference to the English translation by Beveridge, with a slash mark (/) between the two.

Individual Works

IR	*Advertissement tresutile du grand proffit qui reviendroit a la Chrestiente s'il se faisoit inventoire de tous les corps sainctz et reliques* (*Inventory of Relics*); CR 34.
EP	*Epistola Pauli Ad Corinthios I* (*Commentary of the First Epistle of Paul to the Corinthians*); CR 49.
ICR	*Institution de la Religion Chrestienne* (*Institutes of the Christian Religion*); CR 31–32.
NRE	*De Necessitate Reformandae Ecclesiae* (*The Necessity of Reforming the Church*); CR 34.
RS	*Responsio Ad Sadoleti Epistolam* (*Reply to Letter by Cardinal Sadolet*); CR 33.
SR	*Sermon Sur Le Deuteronomy* (*Sermon on Deuteronomy*); CR 54.

Abbreviations

Zwingli

References to Zwingli's work are to the Corpus Reformatorum edition, *Huldreich Zwinglis Samtlich Werke*, Volumes 88–101, edited by Emil Egli and Georg Finsler (Zurich: Theologischer Verlag, 1905ff). My citations from Zwingli follow the abbreviation for the individual work and refer to the volume and pagination of the Corpus Reformatorum. With regard to these individual works, I have used the English translations of Zwingli by Samuel Jackson and Clarence Heller, *Zwingli's Commentary on True and False Religion* (Durham, NC: Labyrinth, 1981), and E. J. Furcha and H. Wayne Pipkin, ed. and trans. *Huldrych Zwingli Writings*, Volumes I and II, (Allison Park, PA: Pickwick Publications, 1984), to accommodate both scholarly and lay readers. Thus, in quotations from Zwingli, my first reference is from the Corpus Reformatorum edition, followed by the English translation source, with a slash mark (/) between the two.

Individual Works

ABN	*Aktion oder Brauch des Nachtmahls* (*Act or Custom of the Supper*); CR 92.
AVC	*Eine Antwort, Valentin Compar gegeben* (*An Answer to Valentin Compar*); CR 91.
CME	*De Canone Missae Epichiresis* (*The Canon of the Mass, Epichiresis*); CR 89.
EML	*Amica exegesis id est: expositio eucharistiae negocii ad Martinum Lutherum* (*Exposition of the Matter of the Eucharist to Martin Luther*); CR 92.
KCE	*Eine Kurze Christliche Einleitung* (*A Short Christian Instruction*); CR 89.
VFR	*De Vera et Falsa Religione Commentarius* (*Commentary on True and False Religion*); CR 90.

Karlstadt

References to the work of Karlstadt are taken from the edition edited by Hans Lietzmann, *Andreas Karlstadt: Von Abtuhung der Bilder*, Kleine Texte für Theologische und Philologische Vorlesungen und Ubungen 74 (Bonn: Marcus & Weber, 1911). The numbers in the text following the abbreviation for *Von Abtu hung der Bylder* (On the Removal of Images) refer to the pagination of this edition. To accommodate both scholarly and lay readers, I have used English translations of Karlstadt's work by Bryan D. Mangrum and Giuseppe Scavizzi, *A Reformation Debate: Karlstadt, Emser, and Eck on Sacred Images, Three Treatises in Translation* (Toronto: The Centre for Reformation and Renaissance Studies, 1991), and also that of E. J. Furcha, *The Essential Carlstadt* (Scottdale, PA: Herald), 1995. Thus, in quotations from Karlstadt, my first reference is from the German edition of Lietzmann, followed by the English translation source, with a slash mark (/) between the two.

Individual Works

VAB   *Von Abtuhung der Bylder* (*On the Removal of Images*)
VGU   *Von Gelubden Unterrichtung* (*Instruction on Vows*)

The Rational Philosophical Consciousness

Introduction: True Religion, Desacralization, and Secularization

PETER BROWN HAS WRITTEN, "THE QUALITY OF A RELIGIOUS SYSTEM depends less on its specific doctrine than on the choice of problems that it regards as important."[1] For the early Protestant Reformed thinkers engaged in the following pages, one issue identified and much debated was the role of material components in the practice and worship of true religion. Calvin elevated this issue into the company of the better known Protestant doctrine of *sola fide*, where the two are judged as the distinctives of Protestantism. Like many other Protestant leaders, Calvin viewed the Lutheran Reformation as leaving unfinished the work of reforming Christian worship. Moreover, much of the Reformed position on the practice of true religion echoed strongly in Zwingli's contention that nothing having to do with the senses could support a spiritual purpose. How the Reformed thinkers evaluated many traditional material components of Christian worship like ritual, icons, and religious art, among other devotional objects and practices, reflects and bears out a largely negative estimation of the value of material components in the practice of true religion.

Furthermore, among a variety of Protestant Reformers, a relationship seems evident in comparing their views of the Eucharist to the place of religious art in religious worship: a parallel pointing to material components of worship as the crucial problem identified in the practice of true religion. One of the more striking parallels to be found among early Protestant Reformers is that, without any significant exception known to me, a

---

1. Brown, *Augustine of Hippo*, 393.

Reformer with a "high" or "low" view of the real presence of Christ in the Eucharist will affirm a correspondingly high or low view of the value of the material elements of religious devotion. One need only compare the views of Luther, Karlstadt, Zwingli, and Calvin to see this similarity, indicating that a common factor in both issues concerns what I refer to in this work as "materiality." Both the Eucharist and the aesthetic have components making or requiring use of the senses, matter, the physical, the tangible, and corroborate that materiality or sensual components have small place in this conception of true religion.[2]

I will compare the views of these sixteenth-century Reformed thinkers on "true religion" to the "philosophical consciousness," the latter a term coined by George Hegel, the nineteenth-century German philosopher. The term was used by Hegel to differentiate between it and a religious mindset or consciousness. For Hegel, religious consciousness and practice attaches to material things—ritual, sacred objects, statuary, art—while the philosophical consciousness frees itself from such things by transcending the need for them. The transition from the religious consciousness to the philosophical also reflects Hegel's view of positive advance in human history; religion is not lost in the philosophical consciousness, but rather realized or consummated by it.

My intent in appropriating Hegel's distinction and evaluation is to frame the arguments of some of the early Reformed theologians over the vexing problem of material components in Christian worship, while offering objections to both Hegel and the Reformed theologians. I will contend that the particulars of the notion of "true religion" by the Reformed theologians bear resemblance to Hegel's spiritualizing philosophical consciousness that impugns the value of religious practice tied to "things." I will argue that in this conception, the path of true religion turns devotees into rational philosophers of a sort, while also arguing that this denuding transformation is effected at significant spiritual expense to Christian worship.

---

2. Michalski, *Reformation*, 168: "Let us start from the end, from the statement that as a rule the opponents of the Real Presence of Christ in the sacrament were supporters of religious aniconism. During the Reformation this pattern was very clear: the views of Luther as a supporter, though moderate, of religious art and of the Real Presence collide here directly with the iconophobia of Karlstadt, Zwingli and Calvin, all of who denied (though in different ways) the Real Presence of Christ in the Host." Similarly, Aston, *England's Iconoclasts*, 7: "It was with natural consistency that those who were most extreme in denying transubstantiation also dealt most radically with images."

The Rational Philosophical Consciousness

Most important to my argument is to indicate how particulars of the Reformed effort to live and practice true religion moved the devotee to work at appreciable distance from the human senses, in the desire for a kind of mental union with God. Mind has a larger role to carry when material components and practices are deemed largely unfit to carry spiritual purpose. By their attenuation or exclusion, a type of monism or mysticism could have resulted from this anthropological and theological shift, but oddly or not, neither came forth in the Reformed tradition, though I would contend, the former does with Hegel. What did follow in the Reformed tradition, nevertheless, comes close to the philosophical consciousness, while also moving the Western world of the sixteenth century closer to the rational modernity of subsequent, though largely secular, centuries.

In Edmund Morgan's book on John Winthrop, *The Puritan Dilemma*, Morgan identified the "dilemma" in his title as the Puritan desire to live in the world without in effect being part of it, because the ultimate calling of the Puritan was to God. The predicament of "true religion" spoken of in these pages, however, ensues by subjugating the senses and the material world in the course of a religious devotion straining to overcome the material components and practices of religious life by largely ignoring or ridding the religious life of them.

The secularization of the West, which in time followed the Reformation critique of the medieval and Catholic view of God and the world, had benefit of the earlier Protestant critique of false religion. The critique of false religion provided important historical impetus to the later, but more severe, secular critique of things religious. These streams of critique of things religious, though obviously different in origin, have prompted the consideration of perhaps a familial congruence between two apparently cultural opposites—one seeking to reestablish in correct form, true religion, and the other attempting to largely remove religion from culture.

A counterargument will insist upon an absolute dichotomy between the two by countering with strong denial of any such relationship between the religious Reformation and nascent modern secular rationalism. Such a contention has plausibility, for the overt conflict with Catholic medieval philosophy mounted by the early Protestant Reformers seems to strongly undermine the suggestion of possible alignment of shared principles between rational religious reformers and conspicuously secular rationalists. The hostility of the latter secularism against religion would seem to provide little possible bridge to the prior historical Reformation effort at reforming wrong religion into right or true religion.

Putting the two in the same direction, however, might be conceivable by interpreting the Protestant Reformation as both slowing and propelling the later secular drift of modern culture. Moreover, in historical hindsight, we not infrequently observe the unintended consequences of an idea spawning unexpected, and even hostile, offspring. Not a few historians have argued for the only apparently odd parallel suggested here, while providing some cogent specifics of the Reformation changes capable of providing some links for a later secular culture that will find itself at odds with some of its Christian, but particularly, Reformed paternity.

As one example, Thomas Molnar, in his book *The Pagan Temptation*, reflects upon the promise, but in addition, the cost of desacrilization in Christianity. He writes, "The tremendous achievement of Christianity, but one that also involved great risks, was the revolutionary proposition of desacralizing the universe and the corresponding concentration of all that is sacred in God."[3] While Molnar attributes much of the impetus of desacralization to Protestantism, in *Sources of the Self*, Charles Taylor further locates some of the strongest push for desacralization within the Protestant Calvinist desire to foster true religion:

> But Protestants and particularly Calvinism classed it [sacralization] with idolatry and waged unconditional war on it. It is probable that the unremitting struggle to desacralize the world in the name of an undivided devotion to God waged by Calvin and his followers helped to destroy the sense that the creation was a locus of meanings in relation to which man had to define himself. Of course the aim of this exercise was very far from forging the self-defining subject, but rather that the believer depends alone on God. But with the waning of Protestant piety, the desacralized world helped to foster its correlative human subjectivity, which now reaped a harvest sown originally for its creator.[4]

As indicated by Taylor, the Reformed desacrilization of nature comes about in the effort at true religion, for in such conception, religious devotion must be jeasously guarded and deemed without competition from anything not God. The medieval grandeur of the things of God—so plentiful so as to be distracting—presented to Protestant critics something like clutter or

---

3. Molnar, *The Pagan Temptation*, 99.
4. Taylor, *Sources of the Self*, 215.

The Rational Philosophical Consciousness

spectacle while detracting from God: the rightful, sole object of worship. Many Protestants judged medieval worship and piety as so much shadow of real things that had already come, though unbeknownst to Catholics gazing as if expectant of something yet to be. In Protestant estimation, Catholic piety had buried the Christian Gospel underneath a suffocating and materialistic religion. Such things as material things were therefore subjected to varying but often severe critiques among Protestant antagonists until, under the severest criticism, few material things had much chance of permitted or continued usage.

This mountain of Protestant critique of medieval Catholic piety has been laboriously studied—though not exhaustively—and so it is far from new to judge the Protestant transformation of religious life and worship as not issuing in great part from a Protestant rational critique of that piety. But paired with the common observation of rationalism inhering in the Protestant critique, it is also common—though less argued than assumed—to believe, along with this, that the strong experiential emphasis in Protestantism diffuses the propensity for rationalism. However, noticeably lacking is an attempt to delineate the blending of these elements. Thus, there is a largely unspecified framework for mapping the rationalist constraints of a Protestant piety insistent on the proper, that is to say, personal or subjective relationship to God. Though this uneasiness between rationalism and the trademark experientialism of Protestantism has been noted by various scholars—some of whose work I will engage in the following pages—few have significantly detailed the nature of this uneasy piety.

My approach in this work is decidedly exploratory with reference to this issue; it is meant to open this issue and subject to new interpretations, rather than cover the subject in any definitive way. My contention, however, is that the aversion to things material is the rudder for understanding much Protestant rational critique of "false religion."

The Self and God

In the more strenuous Protestant forms of the search for true religion, there may be strong resistance to ritual and form in religious worship because of the belief that the human subject must stand by his own subjective understanding in order to truly commune with the object of objective or true worship: God. Religious objects will require good reason for inclusion in this very guarded religious devotion, with the end result often being that the only "helps" for the individual are those the individual commands. That is, the requirement of spiritual authenticity or truthfulness may preclude or separate even the most basic staples of Protestant worship from the worshipper, for a required subjective truthfulness is requisite to their proper use. Evelyn Underhill has perceptively observed as a rigorous example of this notion of authenticity, that in Quakerism, "Here the intense Puritan suspicion of form and demand for a personal religious sincerity [is] so drastic that no word may be said or sung which is not true for each individual worshipper, is pushed to its logical consequence; in the rejection of any kind of organized or premeditated service, even the use of hymns, as likely to involve the violation of 'sensitive truthfulness,' in those who sing but may not always mean them."[5]

This conception of true religion fixes upon the requirement of understanding by the devotee and views that understanding as being impeded, or at least, not advanced by elements of material worship, with communal worship presenting the most difficulty for personal truthfulness. In that context, a worshipper may simply be going along with the crowd when he is one among many in the arena or in the congregation. Therefore, the effort for true worship may drive the communicant into a corner or a closet. Now the focus will be on God and the self, with matter out of the way, though perhaps hardly noticed in its absence.

The paradox of this religious situation is that though beginning with a serious desire to be worshipping God alone and having scoured and rid the path of devotion of impediments, it has as a consequence given pointed attention to the worshipping subject's fittedness for worship. Because of this situation, the subject can now on occasion occupy center stage in the effort to prepare for the worship of God. Thus, for example, it is no accident that the Reformed Puritans, largely critical of the value of art for religious advancement, should be the ones to write, and in fact largely founded, the literary genre of the spiritual autobiography. The aspiring religious subject, however unintended, may now begin to interfere in the desire to not have interfering or distracting material objects, but only God at the center. However, because it is easier to see the self than God, particularly with all "obstacles" removed, the self may be looming larger than ever. In trying to see something other than itself by removing all but the self and the intended God, the subject may see only the self. The bare physical walls of houses of worship, though intended for purposes of "undivided devotion to God,"

---

5. Underhill, *Worship*, 308.

may have the effect of throwing the individual by default upon himself and what resources he commands as his own. This, at least in part, is because the only permitted resource for this finite spirit is the desensualized mind suspicious of material components in spiritual worship.

We might observe that in this effort at "true religion," the focus intended for the object of proper worship, God, turns rather toward a Cartesian-like "turn to the subject" of the next century. Whereas the later secularism of modernity beyond the believing Descartes would argue for independence and autonomy with reference to persons, by contrast, in the Reformed perspective, focus is in earnest directed to God by clearing the required vacancy between God and the worshipper of superfluous things. In this conception, religious concentration is impeded by clutter, or worse, idolatrous clutter. But in the clearing of the space between subject and object to provide enhanced attention and focus toward the object, and in order to "depend on God alone," the objects cleared away in the space between object and subject—and in my study these are material objects—are deemed to serve little to no favorable purpose for religious devotion. This has the radical effect, however, and again, of throwing the worshipper on himself.

However, resistance to negotiating the path to God through any human inventions—as frequently charged by the Reformed thinkers—seems a fundamental resistance toward humanness in the path toward God. In this conception, the human may be anthropologically remade in the likeness of the rational philosopher in order to truly worship God. Meanwhile, the resistance toward humanness ironically causes the human subject to creep to the front, as this aspiring seed for looming modern subjectivity remains firmly planted because the proper spiritual disposition for the subject person is so insisted upon, that in modernity the subject may attract more attention than the sought-for object or God who is deemed no longer there. Yet the reverse was the intention. How could this happen within the Reformed tradition? By way of answer, Killian McConnell has given some indication:

> For Calvin God is always a subject and never an object. In resisting idolatry he is also resisting the attempt to impersonalize or objectify faith, always a danger where religious activity is bound up with things. Personalism is of the essence of the Gospel and without it there is no true faith and no true fellowship with Christ. True knowledge of God is itself personal because persons, God and man, are involved; it is experience because the involvement

is not just intellectual or aesthetic apprehension of an abstraction. True knowledge of God demands and presupposes commitment.[6]

When McConnell makes reference to the Reformed resistance to "impersonalize or objectify faith," he means an undesirable conception of religious objectivity such that the unredeemed subject could utilize it, thus, the necessity of the requirement of "personalism." To exercise faith without the required and pronounced personal relationship to God prominent in Protestantism is illicit. If a religious object provides power to subjects independently of themselves or their subjective state, in the same way, for example, that an inoculation is effective irrespective of the subjective state of the inoculated, then faith can be exercised in the same objective manner, though wrongly. As we will note later, this is one of the primary arguments of prophetic religion against sacramental religion: the religious subject or person in sacramentalism may operate outside of and not within the constraints of the sacramental power of the object that the devotee or subject nonetheless uses and therefore abuses. The subject may use the object without coming to terms with the conditions of rightful object use. Relatedly, the religious subject is oftentimes perceived in Protestantism to derive only as much religious benefit as the subject can understand or negotiate; thus, the *Latin* mass is as unintelligible to the religious subject as the mass itself is idolatrous. According to Rudolf Otto, this shift to a subject-predominated religious life occurs when "The conceptual and doctrinal—the ideal of orthodoxy—began to preponderate over the inexpressible, *whose only life is in the conscious mental attitude of the devout soul*."[7] The importance of the material components of worship are sidelined for the elevated mind lifted above matter.

Another understanding of Reformed Protestant reticence toward the material and sensual elements of religion locates the Reformed judgment of the value of sensual media as an aid in worship, in terms of a genealogy and theology rooted in the prior Hebrew prophetic religious tradition.[8] This is

---

6. McConnell, *John Calvin*, 118.

7. Otto, *Idea of the Holy*, 108. (Italics mine.)

8. Max Weber is a good example. In *The Protestant Ethic*, 105, he writes: "That great historic process in the development of religions, the elimination of magic from the world which had begun with the old Hebrew prophets and, in conjunction with Hellenistic scientific thought, had repudiated all magical means to salvation as superstition and sin, came here to its logical conclusion. The genuine Puritan even rejected all signs of religious ceremony . . . There was not only no magical means of attaining the grace of God . . . Combined with the harsh doctrines of the absolute transcendentality of God and

done with good reason. Calvin, for example, in his essay "The Necessity of Reforming the Church," makes a strong tie between his sixteenth-century reforms for true religion with the Hebrew prophetic religious tradition:

> In regard to doctrine, I maintain that we make common cause with the prophets. For, next to idolatry, there is nothing for which they rebuke the people more sharply than for falsely imagining that the worship of God consisted in external show. For what is the sum of their declarations? That God dwells not, and sets no value on ceremonies considered only in themselves, that he looks to the faith and truth of the heart, and that the only end for which he commanded, and for which he approves them, is, that they may be pure exercises of faith, and prayer, and praise. The writings of all the prophets are full of attestations to this effect. Nor, as I have observed, was there anything for which they laboured more. Now, it cannot, without effrontery, be denied, that when our Reformers appeared, the world was more than ever smitten with this blindness. It was therefore absolutely necessary to urge men with these prophetical rebukes, and draw them off, as by force, from that infatuation, that they might no longer imagine that God was satisfied with naked ceremonies, as children are with shows.[9]

Calvin thus sees his reform indebted to his prophetic predecessors. Particularly, he is emphatic that worshippers not presume their whole duty to God accomplished in "naked ceremonies," but Calvin rarely concedes much value in ceremonies. Like other Reformed thinkers, Calvin presumes that truth is optimally encountered for the worshipper in its barest or "naked" form. Ceremonies weaken and dilute the perception of being in the presence of truth, and therefore afford the worshipper chance to exchange his duty to God in true worship for the motions and glitter of ceremony.

The modern rationalist tradition of the West rising after the Reformation—though of course with mounting secular inclinations—not infrequently concurred to a great degree about the presumed but largely mistaken need for the material world for spiritual purpose. Typical of this viewpoint is a notable passage from Immanuel Kant's 1790 *Critique of Judgement*:

---

the corruption of everything pertaining to the flesh this inner isolation of the individual contains, on the one hand, the reason for the entirely negative attitude of Puritanism to all the sensuous and emotional elements in culture and in religion, because they are of no use toward salvation and promote sentimental illusions and idolatrous superstitions. Thus it provides a basis for a fundamental antagonism to sensuous culture of all kinds."

9. Calvin, *NRE* 6: 477/Beveridge, *Tracts and Treatises*, Vol. I: 151.

Denuded Devotion to Christ

> Perhaps there is no sublimer passage in the Jewish Law than the command, "Thou shalt not make to thyself any graven image, nor the likeness of anything which is in heaven or in earth or under the earth," etc. This commandment alone can explain the enthusiasm that the Jewish people in their moral period felt for their religion, when they compared themselves with other peoples, or explain the pride which Mohammedanism inspires. The same is true of the moral law and of the tendency of morality in us . . . It is quite erroneous to fear that if we deprive this [tendency] of all that can recommend it to sense, it will only involve a cold, lifeless assent and no moving force or emotion. It is quite the other way; for where the senses see nothing more before them, and the unmistakable and indelible idea of morality remains, it would be rather necessary to moderate the impetus of an unbounded imagination, to prevent it from rising to enthusiasm, than through fear of the powerlessness of these ideas to seek aid for them in images and childish ritual.[10]

This passage from Kant, the modern rational moralist, minimizes the role of the sensual element of religion while tolerating religious practice for the moral element. At the same time, he argues that the moral element is capable of standing alone without material support or resonance. He makes essentially unhelpful or even irrelevant, similar to Calvin, a viable connection of support between the material and the moral. For Calvin, the connection between the two is judged to be so fraught with dangers, moreover, that the contention for their severance is frequently positioned within a central argument that one is removed to preserve the health of the other. In other words, the aid to devotion is discarded so as to preserve true devotion.

This devotion, however, will result in the elimination of significant material components, for, *de facto*, cerebral resources of the individual. This is a virtually inevitable outcome given the charge that the sensual and material element is detrimental to the true or moral element of religion. From this perspective, the sensual element is easily conceived of as not only libelous, but manifestly unnecessary, as we see here in Kant.[11]

---

10. Kant, *Critique of Judgement*, 115.

11. This reflects the intertwining of rationalism and Protestant religion. Alexander, "Afterword on Ritual," 220, writes, "The characteristics of ritual rejected by early biblical studies—its bodily, experiential, experimental, and unpredictable qualities—are precisely those features that are of chief interest to Ritual Studies. Early biblical studies could not reconcile these features of ritual with the dualistic perspective of its Protestant and Enlightenment commitments."

The example of Kant, the modern rationalist thinker, though certainly differently religious than thinkers of prior medieval centuries, nonetheless bears some resemblance to the moral emphasis of the prophetic religious tradition with which Calvin identifies his own Protestant reform. Moreover, the emerging rationalism among Reformed Protestant thinkers, as well as modern moralists, seems to inherit some of this impetus from the past Hebraic prophetic tradition. Thus, as frequently pointed out, some Western secular traditions are indebted to significant influence from prior religious beliefs, however adamant growing secular traditions might desire to separate themselves from religion in the present, particularly if it bears unwanted relics of the religious past.

Protestant Doctrine and Protestant Devotion

Within the theological battles fought with Catholicism in the sixteenth century, Protestantism often faulted the weighty and onerous medieval sacramental system for depriving the devotee of access to the mediation of grace in Christ. This failure occurred in Protestant perspective due to an ineffectual conglomerate of specious mediators and erroneous theological understandings present in Catholicism; to Protestants, many of these material objects and practices could never convey and much less absolve the aspirant of his lack of righteousness before God. Moreover, one impetus of Protestantism was to expedite the way to reconciliation with God by removing elements and dubious mediators, evaluated as unnecessary and hence impediments to that goal, such as the quotation from Calvin strongly suggests. But Protestantism has hardly been reductionistic—as is often claimed—for the mere sake of minimalism, however much later Protestantism may have fallen prey to the practice of identifying economy of worship with true worship.

In the final theological analysis, the classical Protestant Reformers felt their justification for the dispute with Catholicism was not only or simply a matter of the immorality of clergy, or other clerical abuses, or even that the Catholic way to God was hopelessly cluttered with wrong things, and perhaps simply wrong for having things—though this is my topic through these pages—but that the Catholic Church embodied wrong doctrine, that is to say, theological errors in the way that it thought about the relationship between God and humans. In the words of Eugene Rice, "Protestants reproached the clergy not so much for living badly as for believing badly, for teaching false and dangerous things."[12]

Many Protestants, moreover, emphasized the vulnerabilities of a ritualistic and materialistic religion that could provide opportunity to negate and substitute the moral requirement of God for ritual niceties and mechanical routine or beautiful aesthetics. Protestants also claimed that absent in much medieval and luxurious ritual was the possibility for a true understanding of the required grace of God necessary for helpless and guilty humans to reach and receive the only hope they have, that is, Christ. What was at particular theological issue for Protestants was a concern for the truth about God and by extension, humans' relationship to God. The moral emphasis and influence of prophetic religion upon Protestantism insisted that God as moral or holy required the human to be no less, and much of Protestantism, following this conviction, insisted that no ritual, no form—nothing but Christ—could meet this otherwise impossible requirement. This is part of the point of Calvin: ritual in and of itself is nothing if it does not serve the proper service. It may on occasion accompany true religion, but will more often imperil it. Hence, one chief suspicion of ritual centers on how it easily unhinges from real religious devotion, thus falling into unknowing ignorance and blasphemous idolatry. Moreover, because a true understanding of God reveals God's exceedingly moral nature, much Protestant understanding of the reconciliation of God and humans advocated the sloughing off of older Catholic practices that Protestants deemed as having buried Christ the Redeemer in mounds of stifling traditions. The Protestant Reformers therefore frequently—and often in droves—took leave of many of the "encumbrances" that they contended made it nearly impossible to see Christ in material worship. Among other versions of Protestant reform, as, for example, the Anabaptists, the eclipse of attention to ritual and the materialistic character of older Christian religious devotion, was oftentimes matched by a fervent moral emphasis, perhaps gaining attention as rituals and the like succumbed to less attention.

William Alston has thus contended that, "we might speculate that the progressive moralization of religion is achieved at the expense of ritual preoccupations."[13] This change, to the degree that it is actually historical, perhaps parallels the most strident route of modern secular thought with insistence on human moral autonomy for proper moral undertaking,

12. Rice, *Early Modern Europe*, 125.
13. Alston, "Religion," 144.

as in Kant. The initial religious faith plays a decreasing role in moral decision-making as morality becomes secularized, where one consequence of this kind of religious "progression" may be the reduction of religion to morality, as it often is in some modern forms of Christianity, where it may be referenced as mere moralism by opponents. Between it and secular morality, there may be only a small difference.

The distinction between the two, moreover, is a distinction with a real and large difference. That is, the reduction of religion to morality has been largely the result of a branch of secular thought respectful enough of religion to respect birthright, but at the same time, reduce and define the essence of religion as morality. A more severe secular ethic, however, will make extra effort to disassociate religious belief entirely from morality so as to achieve "true morality." The orthodox Christian attempt in modernity to keep moral beliefs bound to religious beliefs will confront the more strident secular attempt to take the religious "garb" off morality, with religious morality being evaluated as false morality.

In contrast to the historical and cumulative association of the material element with religion in the form of rituals and other material components, the progression of a moral emphasis within religion, or secular religion, seems to elicit the disciplining of material elements. It is not difficult to envision that in a conception of reformist "true religion," or secular "true morality," religious or moral clarity and understanding may be judged as impeded, or at the very least not expedited or advanced by elements of matter deemed to diffuse the goal of the worshipper seeking moral or godly direction. Coupled with such goals, there may be a push by both toward intellection and away from the senses, given the suspicion toward the material components of religious or moral devotion.[14]

---

14. However, in contrast to the early modern penchant for rationalism, other thinkers have been less applauding than Kant over the effects. As a contrasting example to Kant, Freud leveled severe criticism over the resulting consequences to a religion that spurns the value of the sensual and material. Freud's judgment is noticeably and virtually opposite that of Calvin and Kant. Without implying agreement with Freud's notoriously negative views of anything religious, he writes in *Moses and Monotheism*, 177–79, "Among the precepts of Mosaic religion is one that has more significance than is at first obvious. It is the prohibition against making an image of God, which means the compulsion to worship an invisible God. I surmise that in this point Moses surpassed the Aton religion in strictness. Perhaps he meant to be consistent; his God was to have neither a name nor a countenance. The prohibition was perhaps a fresh precaution against magic malpractices. If this prohibition was accepted, however, it was bound to exercise a profound influence. For it signified subordinating sense perception to an abstract idea; it was

Denuded Devotion to Christ

In many of these changes for assuming proper religious or moral devotion, little notice may be extended toward the human need for symbolism. For example, in Kant, this may even be virtually ignored. For others, moreover, the truth in the ritual, as another example, must be shorn of the circuitous and convoluted form so as to be effectively seen as the truth, for ritual in this criticism is judged as a veil to be removed so as to expose the Real. The Real may be deemed sufficient so as to require no symbolism or resonance with material components because the symbol is judged as less than the reality symbolized or figured by the symbols of faith, for example. With such a path of perceived emancipation taken, religious devotion will become increasingly bare and attentive to the "spiritual" at the expense of the material, or to the inner life as opposed to exterior life, or to the mental over the material.

With the diminishing of such accompaniments to worship like ritual, many early Protestants undoubtedly felt immense and perhaps virtually instantaneous relief, but such freedom in the beginning may exercise too little restraint in what it removes for the future. Indeed, rather than helping or indeed directing the worshipper outside of himself and to God in the displacement of such aid, the devotee is perhaps at risk of losing his way without them. A. N. Whitehead credits both the Reformation and the Scientific Revolution as a time in which "Men tried to dispense with symbols as 'fond things, vainly invented,' and concentrated on their direct apprehension of the ultimate facts."[15]

However, in his chapter on images from the *Institutes*, Calvin, as the central Reformed thinker of the sixteenth century, contends that the voracious human appetite for images, for example, is because "Not contented

---

a triumph of spirituality over the senses; more precisely, an instinctual renunciation accompanied by its psychologically necessary consequence... There opened then the new realm of spirituality where conceptions, memories, and deductions became of decisive importance, in contrast to the lower psychical activity which concerned itself with the immediate perceptions of the sense organs. It was certainly one of the most important stages on the way to becoming human."

15. Whitehead, *Symbolism*, 35. Note again the words of Weber, in note 8, concerning the prophetic responsibility for the demise of ritual "in conjunction with Hellenistic scientific thought." In a more recent work by Auksi, *Christian Plain Style*, the author contends that the plain style ceased when scientific description adopted this type of style for the clarity required in scientific writing. Robert Merton, in his famous work, *Science, Technology and Society*, tried to show that the Puritan type of religiosity, in the attempt to be void of everything but simplicity, served as a natural bridge to modern science and scientific explanation.

with spiritual understanding, they thought that images would give them a surer and nearer impression."[16] In contrast to Calvin, John of Damascus of the Greek tradition of Eastern Christianity, in his ninth-century work, *On the Divine Images*, contends that "Just as words speak to the ear, so the image speaks to the sight. It brings understanding."[17] But for Calvin, the problem is that the sight seeks for an image when it should seek or hear a word. Has God then made any provision for the appetite of sight, or is that appetite simply a thirst for idolatry? According to Calvin's general answer, men have fabricated idols of images because they lacked sufficient spiritual eyes to judge the request ill founded. Speaking of Calvin on this point, David Willis-Watkins has observed,

> One could well expect the argument [God's accommodation] to extend to images: that they are ways God uses to render the Word, preached and celebrated in the sacrament and written, all the more powerfully reinforced through other senses. Calvin's view of accommodation appears in so many dimensions of his thought throughout that his not applying it to images is all the more striking. That is the real heart of the matter for Calvin: the ordinary means consecrated by the Word so intensely grip and sharply affect us that we do not seek other images.[18]

This view, however, would seem to burden any spiritual devotion not so found. That is, guarding worship to such an extent prods the worshipper to nourish himself spiritually from essentially one appetite. In fairness to Calvin and the larger Protestantism, it is apparent on even a cursory reading of Protestant theology, that the experiential element in religious devotion

---

16. Calvin, *ICR* 31: 133/Beveridge, *Institutes,* Book I: 98.

17. John of Damascus, *Divine Images*, 25. Daly, in *God's Altar*, 7, attempts to defend the Puritans against the charge that they had no art, while he nonetheless admits, "To be sure, they were hostile to some forms of art." He concedes, 44, that "They may very well have found their psysic needs overpowering their intellectual prohibitions: that process may well have been the root cause of their art." Interestingly, in speaking of Richard Baxter, perhaps the most famous of the Puritans, Daly comments, 72, on Baxter's famous work, *The Saints Everlasting Rest*, published in 1662, "Where before he had recognized the dangers of idolatry, Baxter now noted the dangers of dealing only in religious abstractions: 'Go to them: When thou settest thyself to meditate on the Joys above, think on them boldly as Scripture hath expressed them: Bring down thy conceiving to the reach of sense . . . Both Love and Joy are promoted by familiar acquaintance: When we go to think of God and Glory in proper conceiving without these spectacles, we are lost and have nothing to fix our thoughts upon.'"

18. Willis-Watkins, "Reform," 48.

is deemed absolutely essential as noted earlier. The question, however, is whether a view that distances the human senses from spiritual engagement amplifies or encumbers communion with God for the human.[19] Moreover, from Calvin's point of view, one might judge that true religion is in perpetual peril due to human anthropology. In the individual's propensity to desire God—not of course an evil desire for Calvin—the person compensates for a presumption of absence and the need for presence by making visual gods that fail, while providing an idolatrous and illusory sense of the presence of God. Idolatrous propensities proceed to fill the religious life with things which will fill life but will not fulfill, as idolatry increases. The question, however, is whether putting the devotee on a unitary track for communion with God need meet with more than human minds in human lives.

The rationalist propensity for a predominant use of the verbal sensibility is thereby strengthened in such religious culture, in part because the invisible spirit is perceived best articulated and identified with words. Traditionally, of course, in Protestantism, God has been present in His Word. But the original meaning of the Word of God may now largely and literally mean words so as to avoid idolatry elsewhere; much of the desire of the historic Protestant reform of religious practice in the sixteenth century was to remove perceived unnecessary and idolatrous mediations poised between God and persons. However, the purging of the material from religious worship also truncated the levels on which one could appropriate religious truth to a singular and often solitary level of the intellect. With sensuous mediums now spurned or condemned, the communion with God must increasingly turn to the intellect and its chief mediums, words and language. This historical state roughly corresponds to Hegel's famous sentence from his *Introduction to Aesthetics*: "Yet, precisely, at this highest stage, art now transcends itself, in that it forsakes the element of a reconciled embodiment of the spirit in sensuous form and passes over from the poetry of the imagination to the prose of thought."[20]

Notably, the odyssey of the human finite spirit in search of communion with the materially invisible Spirit or God begins to resemble the

---

19. Partee, *Calvin and Classical Philosophy*, 51, ventures that "Calvin's view of man is perhaps more indebted to the insights of the philosophers than any other area of his thought." He goes on to write, 64, "It might be argued that Calvin 'had a spiritualizing tendency' and that Luther was more sensitive to the Biblical antithesis of flesh and spirit as distinct from body and soul . . . Perhaps Calvin over-reacts to the Anabaptists, Osiander, Servetus, and Socinus, but he firmly believes that both soul and body are from God."

20. Hegel, *Introduction to Aesthetics*, 89.

progressive realization of Spirit in history in Hegel's philosophy. The attenuation of physical components as having only temporal parts to play Hegel applauds as historical progression, because in the realization of their limitation, the philosophical consciousness begins to work in independence from material entities. Material things turn out to be paltry spiritual companions by comparison to spiritual things. However, for the person not desirous of the elevation to the cerebral satisfactions of the philosopher, nor possessing a perennial penchant for the things of the mind to the virtual exclusion of the things of the senses, the Christian God may seem captive to the god of the philosophers under a philosopher's regimen.[21]

However, in Hegel's historical assessment of such a change of consciousness and cultural history, philosophical consciousness shows the weakness of the prior need for the pictorial and imagistic cognition of art and religion as the philosophical consciousness approaches the highest mode of knowing and being.[22] Any difficulty created by the absent material components and rituals in the worship and understanding of God is in Hegel's conception a necessary and higher movement, prompting the devotee to take his knowledge to a higher level.[23] For Hegel, the finite spirit is diminishing not only the distance between itself and the Infinite, but the difference, by a receding of the sensual in deference to the spiritual.[24] In Hegel's mind, this is an advance over the practice of sacramental religion. There the human was and still is moved "backwards" to the sensual and

21. An excessive or exclusive use of the verbal sensibility, however, can perhaps contribute to lowering the conception of the transcendence and majesty of God—Calvin's concern against the use of sensual images—because the ease of the medium contributes to a complacent familiarity with the object of the medium. C. S. Lewis makes a similar point in regard to the Evangelical tradition in Protestantism in his *Letters to Malcolm*, 13, "I think the 'low' church *milieu* that I grew up in did tend to be too cosily at ease in Zion. My grandfather, I'm told, used to say that he 'looked forward to having some very interesting conversations with St. Paul when he got to heaven.' Two clerical gentlemen talking at ease in a club! It never seemed to cross his mind that an encounter with St. Paul might be rather an overwhelming experience even for an Evangelical clergyman of good family. But when Dante saw the great apostles in heaven they affected him like *mountains*." (Italics in the original.)

22. As example, Hegel writes in his *Introduction to the Lectures on the History of Philosophy*, 62, "But, strictly speaking, philosophy's topic is God alone, or its aim is to know God. This topic it has in common with religion but with this difference, namely that religion treats the subject pictorially while philosophy thinks and comprehends it."

23. Ibid., 166, "All err who assume that the unity of spirit with nature is the most excellent mode of consciousness. On the contrary, this stage is the lowest, the least true . . ."

24. On this point Hegel is far different from the Reformed thinkers.

Denuded Devotion to Christ

to material reality, whereas philosophical consciousness propels the finite spirit forward by moving away from the material to the infinite Spirit. The religious consciousness, however, can get stuck in time and matter, and, consequently, not move forward to the spiritual satisfactions of the philosophical consciousness.

I am contending that the effort expended toward true religion within Reformed Protestantism provides at least a rough example of a religion poised toward the philosophical consciousness in Hegel's schema. Moreover, the disappearance of the sensual from religious practice and devotion, I regard as mistaken, though such exclusions seem commensurate with Hegel's scheme of the progressive historical transition from religious materialism to philosophical conceptualization. However, incommensurate with the Protestant perspective is Hegel's proclivity toward monism, despite his own affirmation of Protestantism. More compatibility between Hegel and the Reformed thinkers is evidenced in their mutual aversion to mysticism. The most compatibility between them, therefore, is in their notion that the sensible material world serves the spiritual world and devotion most when the latter takes leave of the former. For both, the material seems to constitute an obstacle to the spiritual.

The Flesh and the Spirit

Many of the theological issues associated with materiality in Protestantism arise over the "means of mediation." (In Puritanism, the terminology would be "means of grace.") Any suggestion of some "thing" possibly perceived as a mediator besides Christ was rejected as idolatrously displacing Christ as the sole mediator between God and persons. Thus, there arises the suspicion of anything that could possibly be seen as another competitor to Christ. Typical of this caution is a passage in Howard L. Rice's *Reformed Spirituality*: "The Reformed tradition has always been deeply concerned about the dangers of idolatry. Efforts to achieve special experiences for ourselves easily fall into the trap of being idolatrous. People can get caught up in the desperate need to imagine a god of their own and strive to make sure they have sensations that will reinforce their images. People who are overeager to seek out the unusual may miss the God of the ordinary."[25]

This insistence, however, almost dispenses with the "God of the ordinary." Indeed, the worshipping subject may object that by removal of such aids to devotion, he inherits the risk of feeling further away from Christ than

25. Rice, *Reformed Spirituality*, 37.

The Rational Philosophical Consciousness

before. Hence, the Christ with whom one is to experience reconciliation with God by redemption may actually seem more distant by ushering God too quickly onto the metaphysical plane. But at this juncture, the objection may be raised that one does not fabricate or reformulate his theology on the basis of the senses. However, the point is that with this exclusion, and others like it, the devotee must begin to negotiate his religion rather in the manner of the stereotypical philosopher notorious for living in his head.[26]

The goal perhaps is to aspire to an imageless truth, and not a mere image, for images, like symbols, intervene or mediate between ourselves and the "Real," and thus are for that reason objectionable.[27] But with all images removed, one can feel rather at a loss than a gain. With great irony, the imageless truth may begin to look dimmer than the image. This is not, however, because the imageless truth is weak, but because *we* are.

The details in this conception of true religion, however, are noticeably not those of accommodation to human weaknesses, but the presupposition that our sufficiency is in the strength of the only true Mediator, that is, Christ. But if the judgment of this kind of religious experience as inordinately straining the communicant is essentially correct for some of the reasons here suggested, then at least some of the sensual mediations employed in religious practice appear not simply as Gregory the Great intimated about images—only concessions to the unlearned—but helps needed perhaps by the learned as well.[28] Their exclusion is manifest in

---

26. Hegel writes in his *Introduction to the Lectures on the History of Philosophy*, 28: "Art and religion are the modes in which the Absolute Idea is present for non-philosophical people, creatures of feeling, perception, pictorial thinking." Adding to this, 31, he writes: "But this form, whereby the absolutely universal content belongs to philosophy alone, is the form of thinking, the form of the universal itself. But in religion this content is given (through art) to the direct vision of things outside, and then to pictorial thinking and feeling." A typical passage in which Hegel articulates the movement to the "naked truth" of philosophy is the following, 35–36: "The eternal reason, as logos, as declaring, expressing, and revealing itself, does reveal itself, therefore, in our soul and ideas, and only for that reason to our soul and ideas, to our sensitive consciousness, reflecting naively on what it receives. Further and more abstract reflection begins to regard this shape and mode of thinking as a veil behind which the truth is supposed to be hidden and concealed, and then tries to strip this veil away from what lay behind it and to bring out the truth, pure, naked, as it genuinely and really is."

27. This goal is predicated on assuming we can have a pure, naked spirituality. Farrer, in his *Rebirth of Images*, 81, writes, ". . . it is a mistake to suppose that spirituality came naked into the world, or could exist without the images that condition it."

28. Pope Gregory the Great's famous statement that "Images are the books of the unlearned" set an important precedent for the use of images in Medieval Catholicism,

the existential ramification of excluding portions of human sensibility for nearly complete insistence upon the verbal sensibility. The Protestant belief in the Augustinian doctrine of human depravity finds itself ironically in league with an elevated view of the human capability for spiritual devotion. With a minimum of or exclusion of material components for spiritual purpose, and serious disciplining of the human senses, one may have to fall back on oneself for spiritual advance. That self will be a mind or a spirit.

The *locus classicus* of the contention that true religion occurs within the spirituality of worship was often the biblical reference arising from the response of Christ on the question of the "place" of worship to the Samaritan woman at the well: "An hour will be coming, and now is, when true worshippers will worship the Father in spirit and in truth; for such are the people the Father desires as worshippers. God is spirit and those worshipping Him must worship in spirit and truth."[29] This passage Hegel quotes frequently in his writings. The use of this verse, also prominent in iconoclastic circles during the Iconoclastic Controversy of the eighth century, necessitates that one scrutinize where the preference for "spiritual" as opposed to material worship more precisely lies in Protestantism.

The Platonic aversion to the physical may provide some undercurrent of resistance to the material, and Plato's incorporation into early Christian anthropology was due, among other reasons, to a metaphysic that viewed the human as a soul in the prison of a material, and thankfully for platonists, a mortal body. This view was historically treated with more comparisons than contrasts to Christian anthropology and theology in the Medieval period, and up to the present it continues to influence Christian thinking. However, though the aversion to the "flesh" in Plato has reference to the real corporeal body as the vehicle which can enslave and subdue the spirit or soul for its own fleshly purposes, Christians sometimes used Plato's contrasts as if they were identical in meaning with their own. However, the deliverance of the soul or salvation for Plato can never be ultimately resolved as long as the two are in union. Platonism and "spiritual" Christianity thus have a very uneasy relationship—appearances to the contrary.

---

though one heavily criticized by the Protestant Reformers in general. However, for however much Gregory's statement sanctioned the use of images and art for religious devotion, he can also be seen as perhaps circumscribing physical symbols as merely temporal needs of the unlearned, and thus in a sense tying these devotional aids to a pre-literate stage of human culture.

29. Gospel of John 4:3–4, my translation.

In Christian and New Testament theology, the "flesh" there denounced as inimical to the progress of the spiritual life is not Plato's physical and material "flesh." The flesh in the New Testament is a metaphor for the evil nature of the fallen human being in his decrepit and helpless human nature perhaps aspiring but failing to follow Christ. Moreover, in the Christian religion, the Incarnation of Christ is one instance—though a very powerful one—of decisively displacing the Platonic estimation of the central problem of the human predicament. Plato could never be a sacramentalist with his view of the physical world. Many Protestants, to avoid too much closeness to something like sacramentalism, at least of the medieval sort, have courted their religious practice close to the Platonic conception, but with some jeopardy to their Christian beliefs.

Plato's vision of the relationship between the human soul and body clearly bears out the significant difference with the Christian conception. Plato might fittingly be described as a loose and recalcitrant dualist, for he aspires toward a monistic spirit metaphysic and a spiritualized human anthropology. This means that he believes the human is a soul and a body, but he resents the presence of the body for its numerous and negative impacts upon the soul. Therefore, there is a grave hostility between the two in Plato's conception, best exemplified in his description of the body as the prison of the soul. The relationship between the two, therefore in principle, is antagonistic, for the soul, encumbered as it is with the afflictions of the body, must assert its mastery over the powerful but temporary prison, though from considerable disadvantage to the prisoner while the body lives, for the embodied prison binds the hapless soul to itself. At its worst, the consequential desires of the body blind the unseeing soul to the point that the body so overwhelms the subjugated and weakened soul, that the human may eventually cease to recognize the presence or even the existence of a soul because it has been so effectively muted or silenced by a domineering mastery of the human by the body.

As similar as this conception of Plato may seem at points to the Christian conception of the warfare of flesh and spirit, the two conceptions are in fact only distantly related, though they are often conflated by Christians of various historical epochs and various communions and confessions. The absolute difference is perhaps best highlighted in noting the dignity that the Christian conception of the human person gives to the body, in contrast to Plato's punitive conception that the body is a prison. Still greater, however, is the dignity that the Christian conception of the material world conveys upon that world at large: a material world that Plato finds offensive to spiritual purpose. The attitude of Plato toward the material world shows that indeed the rivalry between flesh and spirit is irresolvably that, for he conceives of the two as in principle impossibly opposed, whereas in Christianity, again, the conflict of flesh and spirit depicts the antagonism between good and evil found in the embattled human person. In other words, in Christianity, the defining human problem is not that we have flesh or a body made of matter, but what we have done with our flesh and our body—as well as our soul or spirit. The sins of each evidence that our culpability to fail on both fronts is formidable. But our real problem is not simply eliminated by eliminating the body, because the presence of the body is not the ultimate fount or source of our human problem or predicament. Sin issues not from matter, *qua matter*, and thus we are not sinful because matter is sinful as matter; therefore, we can hardly claim exemption from sin by exempting ourselves from matter.

Indeed, the falling away of the body at physical death creates almost insuperable difficulties for the Christian conception of the human person, in contrast to Plato, for whom the Christian resolution of the reunion of the two would in his mind, simple repeat the besetting problem. That is, the disunion of the soul and the body at bodily death creates a catastrophe for the Christian conception of the human person, for the human person is a union of body and soul. The separation between them precipitated by bodily death, therefore, is in a sense as unnatural as it is real, for it breaks the human person into two parts that are meant to be conjoined and united, not separated, as they are by the physical death of the body. The Platonic conception of the human person, however, has no such quandary, calamity, or grief over bodily death, for the source of the human problem dies with the material body; for Christians, however, this "solution" is no gain, but a grievous loss. It would come as a contradiction to the Christian conception. Plato's lowly estimation of the body and the material world that God created is noticeably different from the Christian estimation.

In short, Christians are taking Plato as a dubious consort in devaluing the material form in which God found it fit to make humans and which God, in Christ, took upon himself. Indeed, the resurrected human person after death is restored to the union of soul, and this time, an imperishable body. In other words, the Christian resurrection of the body attests to that part of us as a rightful part of us, such that a restoration of the body to the widowed and floundering and famished soul apart from the human body is necessary for the full complimentary nature of the human—as a soul and a body. Thus, we are truly fearfully and wonderfully made, but in physical death we are unmade by the parting of our material body. In Platonism, however, effort is made in trying to pry apart in life what will be apart when the solo spirit reveals the real person in a permanent condition of absence from the body. But in Christianity, God in Christ reunites the two in the resurrection of the body; thus, it would be disparaging to God to try to separate what God rejoins together after death, but also seamed together in life. Despite protest against the incorporation of formal philosophy into theology at the time of the Reformation, Protestantism has had at times its own subtle—and sometimes not so subtle—undercurrent and sometimes floodwaters of Platonism fueling grievances and opposition to the material.

Human Nature and Protestant Devotion

Patrick Henry has made the point that two fundamentally different religious anthropologies are in disagreement over what constitutes proper religious worship for true religion, particularly with regard to the appropriateness of material components in that worship:

> For both the Iconoclast and the Iconodule, worship is an activity in which man gets closer to the divine. The iconoclast believes that in order to do that, it is necessary to relegate humanity to the background. We can be assured of our kinship with God only insofar as we leave our humanity behind. The Iconodule, on the contrary, believes that our approach to God is specifically through our humanity. Man was made in the image and likeness of God; not the soul (psyche) or the mind (nous) but man (anthropos). Worship is the activity not of the man who has transcended his humanity, but of the man whose humanity is restored. The paradigm for worship in spirit and in truth is not the angels in heaven, but Adam and Eve in paradise . . . The Iconoclasts imply that all you need for proper worship is a pure mind.[30]

This contrast prompts the question that must be raised at some point about the feasibility of, in effect, disrobing God and the devotee down to spirits for proper religious devotion and worship. Is this not perhaps a fantastic notion—that is, an idealized or utopic conception—where only

---

30. Henry, "Iconoclastic Controversy," 27–28.

perfected worshippers in the correct frame of mind could uphold this kind of worship? Accordingly, Margaret Aston writes:

> Were those who tried so hard to break this 'crust of formality' attempting the impossible? Could worshippers really find 'all comfort' in the bare communion of the word? Was it true, as Calvin asserted, that 'most ceremonies have no other use than to numb the people rather than to teach them'? Or that faith, as Milton claimed, had no need of 'the weak, and fallible office of the senses as ushers, or interpreters, of heavenly mysteries' except in the sacraments? Were believers, like God, really best pleased with the worship that had the least admixture of human aids?[31]

On this very question, Steven Ozment has speculated about some possible reasons for the "failure" of the Reformation: "Its failure rather lay in its original attempt to ennoble people beyond their capacities—not as medieval theologians and Renaissance philosophers had done, by encouraging them to imitate saints and angels, but by demanding that they live simple, sober lives, prey not to presumption, superstition, or indulgence, but merely as human beings. This proved a truly impossible ideal; the Reformation foundered on man's indomitable credulity."[32]

This analysis stumbles over identifying what is needful for the "human." That is, one may agree that sectors of the Protestant Reformation asked religious practitioners to exercise what would seem to amount to a philosophical as opposed to a religious consciousness—by making little use of the components of material religion. If this were the failure of the Reformation, then failure is hardly to be judged as due to "man's indomitable credulity." Furthermore, if it proved to be a "truly impossible ideal" to live "merely as human beings," then the nature of human beings is up for question. That is, is it a failure of human nature or a failure of religious practice that ignores human nature that provides the reason for the failure of the Reformation?

Interestingly, in another work, Ozment concedes something of this point:

> The limited appeal of Protestantism, existentially and intellectually, is not difficult to explain and should have been expected. Traditional Catholic piety and folk beliefs are far older and richer religious systems. They are arguably more emotionally involving

---

31. Aston, *England's Iconoclasts*, 12–13.
32. Ozment, *Age of Reform*, 438.

for their adherents. They also accommodate human frailty and folly more conscientiously and with greater enterprise than their Protestant counterparts. The devotion to the continuity of the world of the living with that of the dead, the predictable cycle of sin and forgiveness, the breathtaking shrines and sparkling festivals, the sensuous, tangible piety—all these things make traditional religion more enticing for the devout layperson and curious ethnographer alike. Protestant faith by comparison has seemed all too simple and austere a religion, the spiritual equivalent of a sobering cold bath.[33]

That the results following a denuded devotional model "should have been expected" seems a legitimate and fair complaint against blindness or utopianism of perhaps the most strident Protestant Reformers. However, the presumption in Ozment's prior analysis seems to be that image use, pilgrimages, and use of relics, as examples, are indeed signs of human weakness or credulity (as in Zwingli, Calvin, and Hegel), while nonetheless claiming that the Reformation asked persons to live "merely as human beings." The issue is that the Reformed conception, as an example, delimits creaturely aids for devotion, which, in Ozment's words, describes people living "merely as human beings." However, the Reformed conception of true religion seems to prod religious devotion to stretch outside the mold of the human being, while making a way toward God as bodiless spiritual beings, as noted by Henry. These humans live not "merely as human beings," but as another kind of being, and not as a restored Adam or Eve. However, this presupposes that for proper religious devotion, humans must take on the modality of the spiritual God—to accommodate themselves to something like the "god of the philosophers." God in history, however, in the Incarnate Christ, took on the modality of the human being.

The fate of the point of Ozment is somewhat like Bertrand Russell's quip that if one formulates an ethic that ignores human nature, then chances are that human nature will ignore that ethic. One can of course blame either term in the equation for the failure. Generally speaking, moreover, one might suggest that Catholicism blames the failure of Protestantism on ignoring human nature, while Protestantism blames the failure of Catholicism on capitulating to a flawed human nature. Either way raises the question not just of the nature of human nature, but of the role and *legitimacy* of human nature in Christian religious life and worship. The seeming

---

33. Ozment, *Protestantism*, 215.

assumption in the argument of Ozment is that there is a weakness in human nature that made the success of the Reformation attempt at riddance of images, rituals, pilgrimages, etc., virtually impossible. With this is the suggestion of an inflated idealism in a Reformation call for the impossible. And yet, according to Ozment, the Reformation call was to live "merely as human beings." On the other hand comes the suggestion that people cannot simply or stoically bear the separation from all they threw out as refuse or unnecessary clutter. The central problem is compounded, moreover, when worshippers are being called to worship as elevated spiritual beings, when they are in human form with bodies and souls.

From the perspective of this writer, it seems fair to ask if it is an affront to God to reinvent ourselves as bodiless beings while also devising a spiritual ladder for our spirit for communion with God. The necessity for grace is clearly understood in the primary salvific doctrines of Reformation Protestantism, but on the issue of "the rest," many sectors of Protestantism hesitate, feeling the threat of compromise to the Protestant doctrine of salvation.

There is, moreover, sometimes, and paradoxically, a tempting spiritual pride derived from the apparent emancipation from material and other devotional aids unneeded by the spiritually mature who concede little place for matter in spiritual worship. Ozment speaks of the double-sidedness of this truncated Protestant devotion:

> Many found themselves relieved of much burdensome conventional piety. But the Reformation also posed a new and different spiritual threat for the laity. Although Protestantism had simpler religious rituals, each had suddenly become absolute, its importance enhanced by the reduction of religion to a claimed vital core. This raised the stakes spiritually for devout believers. The slack had gone out of religion, but with it went also, as the passage of time confirmed, some of the familiarity and comfort. The reformers in the end created a version of what they had originally vehemently opposed: an elite religion . . . It was a religion for any and all who could forego the sweet deceits of traditional piety.[34]

This, of course, is the Protestant living "merely as a human being." The liability of such a position, however, will be in construing human beings, not as material beings but as aspiring disembodied spirits, while faulted and scorned religious practices may nevertheless reflect some real but

---

34. Ibid., 216.

stringently resisted human desires that Christian religious devotion may dismiss too quickly. This may occur when religious devotion begins to finesse religious understanding at too much distance from material elements for material beings following Christ.

The Reformed perspective has thus perhaps accurately been described as a "purely intelligible affair to the exclusion of the senses."[35] In many ways, this requires something of an application of Ockham's razor applied to the devotional religious life. Horton Davies, commenting upon the later Reformed Puritans' religious worship writes, "There were no processions, bowings, crossings, or other gestures; no responses to keep attention during the longer prayers. In short, there was hardly any concession made to human psychology or to the delight of the ear or the eye. This was the most economical simplicity imaginable . . . It was a highly vertebral worship . . ."[36]

Margaret R. Miles, in speaking of Calvin has written the following:

> But his short discussion of private ascetic practice in the Institutes 4.12 gives no indication that Calvin recognized the value of "exercises" involving the body to collect psychic energy. Even the insight of Augustine—with which Calvin was familiar—that physical asceticism directly transfer to the preparation of a particular state of soul has not outweighed in his mind the more immediate antagonism he felt toward the traditional ascetic practices advocated by the Roman church. The only value he acknowledges in the two practices he mentions—fasting and sexual abstinence—is their usefulness for aiding public and private prayer by a "disencumbered" mind. Predictably, Calvin emphasizes that public repentance requires and depends on "a feeling of the mind" which precedes and naturally results in "external manifestations." . . . For Calvin the capacity of the soul to affect the body is not matched by any capacity of the body to affect the soul. The body remains "motion devoid of essence."[37]

Notably, Calvin sees in the first five centuries of Christianity a commendable refrain from his perception of the later excesses of art, icons, and sensibility by the Church. This viewpoint is confirmed by Miles' statement in her *Fullness of Life: Historical Foundations for a New Asceticism*: "By the sixth century, people were no longer fascinated by the orderly and trustworthy hierarchical arrangement of human being and cosmos, but rather

---

35. Miles, *Image as Insight*, 87.
36. Davies, *American Puritans*, 274–75.
37. Miles, "Calvin on the Body," 318.

by the way in which the incarnation acted as a model of the activity of God in the sensible world."[38] However, the shift of religious devotion from the sensible to the transcendent that "demanded that spiritual reality be sought *above* the things of this earth, not *in* them"[39] found its home too often in a kind of Platonic rationalism. True religion, in this shift, however, may with more historical time become predominantly, if not exclusively ethics—as it does in many modern liberal Christian communities—and in so doing, provides some parallel to the movement of modern Western history. In that historical advance, religion is increasingly subsumed into morality—thus largely reversing the relationship of the two from the Christian medieval conception. The Christian religion in the modern period may be equated with morality and nothing more. However, it may move even further afield by contending that the Christian religion has no message at all for modern man, or at least not one that cannot be supplied in essential import by secularism.

---

38. Miles, *Fullness*, 82.
39. Eire, *War*, 44.

Karlstadt, Zwingli, and Calvin on True Religion

Reformed Rejection of Materiality in the Practice of True Religion

IN THIS CHAPTER I WILL EXAMINE THE THOUGHT OF KARLSTADT (1480–1541), Zwingli (1484–1531), and Calvin (1509–1564), to highlight aspects of how the religious devotion of true religion conceptualized the religious practitioner and God. Though the Reformed thinkers did not speak with the terminology of distinguishing between religious and philosophical consciousness, they often wrote of the difference between true and false religion. The difference between a right religion and a wrong religion for them often revolved around the issue of tangible, visible, and material elements in religious devotion. The issues involved over these elements were mammoth. As noted by Peter Auksi,

> When the first reform-minded students of church history and practice turned in the first half of the sixteenth century to review the scriptural warrants behind inherited liturgy, *they were in effect redefining a complex group of questions and emphases, involving the nature of true worship, the nature of the deity worshipped, and the strength of all impediments to their renewed, regenerate approach to him. Their efforts in redefinition constituted a sporadic revival of many centuries of formal inquiry into the means by which inward motive, sensuous circumstance and scriptural authority could or should influence the relationship between the believer and his God.*[1]

---

1. Auksi, "Simplicity and Silence," 356–57. (Italics mine.) Also to be noted is the statement of Limouris in his *Icons*, 78, "Iconoclasm was not the work of individual fanatical demagogues, but *the expression of a deep revolution in piety.*" (Italics mine.)

Denuded Devotion to Christ

The issue of tangible, visual, and material elements of worship first became a decisive issue in the Reformation in the clash between Andreas Karlstadt and Martin Luther. Though Luther criticised Karlstadt's position severely in his *Against the Heavenly Prophets*, Karlstadt's position on material devotion also drew criticism from Catholics. Johannes Eck, though Luther's principal Catholic theological opponent, also attacked the position of Karlstadt on the particular point of images in religious worship, as had Luther.[2] Eck would also later be summoned by Swiss Catholics to debate the radical reform of religious devotion by Ulrich Zwingli, with whom Luther himself insisted on sharp disagreements over many of the same points. Thus, it is not strange to witness Catholics and Lutherans at a later period on occasion working in league against the Reformed position on the issue of material aids in religious devotion.

In a letter of 1524, Luther indicates the similarity of the "spiritualist" position of Karlstadt to Zwingli and beyond by writing that "Carlstadt's poison crawls far. Zwingli at Zurich . . . and many others have accepted his opinion . . ."[3] For Luther, the mistake of Karlstadt and Zwingli in their redefinition of true religion could be seen in their haste to get by matter and on to spirit. As an example, Luther remarked in his treatise on Karlstadt: "The inward experience follows and is effected by the outward. God has determined to give the inward to no one except through the outward."[4] In Luther's view, Karlstadt and Zwingli mistakenly minimized the material vehicles by which God as spirit comes to humans. Luther refused to see the road to spirit expedited by a kind of leap frog religious devotion.[5]

Karlstadt lost his fight with Luther over the issue of material objects of religious devotion in Wittenberg and in the subsequent Lutheranism.

---

2. Eck, *On Not Removing Images of Christ and the Saints*, 1523.

3. Letter of Luther to Nicholas von Amsdorf, 2 December, 1524. Quoted in Gerrish, *Reformation*, 59.

4. Luther, *Against the Heavenly Prophets*, 146.

5. Bainton, in his *Erasmus*, 215, writes that "Erasmus himself had referred to the Mass as a mystical sign, a memorial of Christ's death, the bond of believers with each other and with their Lord, and a commitment to follow in his steps. The mere corporeal presence of Christ, said he, is useless for salvation. The eating of his flesh and the drinking of his blood are worthless unless in the spirit. The sacrament is a celestial food in which Christ is present beneath the bread and the wine. *For all the variations, this was basically the position of Carlstadt . . . basically the position of Zwingli . . . This group wished to sweep away all of the external practices, to remove the images, smash the organs, reduce the Mass to a very simple Lord's Supper . . . For all their spiritualizing they were in danger of a new externalism of reductionism.*" (Italics mine.)

That specific loss, however, would turn into victory in other religious communities of the Protestant Reformation. The historical irony in Karlstadt's defeat is that even though he was banished from Wittenberg by Luther for suspected association with violent iconoclasm in that city, Karlstadt's position on external and material religion did indeed begin to "crawl," and in gaining strength elsewhere, it would eventually find its way into large sectors of Protestantism both within and beyond the Reformed tradition.

However, Karlstadt and his theological successors did not invent a new issue in the history of the Christian church, for the use of material objects for religious devotion had not escaped objections and conflict, oftentimes intense, in the history of the Christian church. The Protestant Reformers seized upon the history of this conflict. In an attempt to convey an historical lack of concensus on the use of material aids, they noted the strong objections of some early Christian thinkers and theologians, such as Vigilantius and Lactantius, and the lesser reservations expressed by Augustine and Jerome.[6]

The Reformed thinkers, moreover, most exploited the range of the conflict over images that had arisen in the East in the famous Iconoclastic controversy, for the Eastern affirmation of images was not wholly shared by the Western Church, even though the religious culture of the West increasingly shared in the use of images and other material components in religious devotion. The counterpart to the huge Iconoclastic Controversy in the Eastern Church during the eighth and ninth century[7] surfaced in the Western Church during the reign of the Frankish king Charlemagne (c. 742–814). Because of the increase of "visible" as compared to "spiritual" worship, Charlemagne's court theologians began to ponder the propriety of the use of images and relics in Christian devotion. These theologians produced, around 790, the *Libri Carolini*, which, among other contentions, was generally negative toward religious imagery. When this work was

---

6. For example, Calvin: "Moreover, let Lactantius and Eusebius be read on the subject . . . In like manner, Augustine distinctly declares, that it is unlawful not only to worship images, but to dedicate them" (*ICR* 31: 126/ Beveridge, *Institutes,* Book I: 95).

7. Pelikan, in his *Imago Dei*, 7, speaks of the two sides in that controversy as the Christian idealists and Christian materialists: "By the time of the Iconoclastic Controversy, therefore, the 'Christian idealism' that was so prominent especially in the thought of many of the Alexandrian church fathers such as Clement of Origen had been counterbalanced by what could no less legitimately be styled a 'Christian materialism.'" I have labeled the implied ontology held by 'Christian idealism' as "naked truth," while differentiating the latter position from the mystical notion of divine truth that can come too close to religious monism for Protestant comfort.

republished in 1549, Reformed thinkers not unnaturally seized upon it for their own arsenal. Calvin in particular saw the work as an early attempt by the Frankish church to extricate itself from the errors of false religion. However, until the document received attention from the Protestant Reformers, the *Libri Carolini* had been a neglected work in an era immersed in material religious devotion.

Only outwardly accepting the dictum of Gregory the Great (c. 540–604) that images are the "books of the unlearned," the *Libri Carolini* contrasted the spirituality of the Scriptures with the material nature of the image and the relic: "the rudimentary and physical quality of the Byzantine rites is contrasted with the spirituality of the Scriptures: it is pointed out that God gave *written* laws to Moses; that the prophets *wrote*, did not paint, as the evangelists had done before them, that the Apostles *spoke* and *preached*."[8]

Moreover, Scavizzi notes that a rational consciousness underlay many of the criticisms of material religion in the *Libri Carolini*, however submerged and largely ignored the objections were in the intervening medieval period before the Reformation. However, they would resonate in the reform of religious devotion by the Reformed thinkers: "The *Libri* reached a paradoxical conclusion which would be echoed by [John] Foxe a few years after their [re]publication: Christians had been more idolatrous than pagans; as a consequence, the *Libri* invoked a radical change in the quality of spiritual life. The Western tradition could identify with these statements. As in the eight century the Frankish Church expressed her rationalist roots against the 'sacramental magic' of the Byzantine Church, the Western world now emancipated itself from the magic fetters imposed by the Roman Church."[9]

In the words of Anthony Ugolnik, the *Libri Carolini* can be assessed as" heralding a distinctly Western and critical consciousness . . . they represent a trend in the West which anticipates the Reformation."[10] At the time of its initial publication, however, and in the subsequent historical period, the *Libri* had little influence. It was largely forgotten until the Reformed thinkers, upon its republication, began to use it to such an extent that the work was placed on the Catholic Index.

The spiritualistic tenor and arguments of the *Libri Carolini* stood neglected in the *cultus divorum* of the medieval period, but in time, an

---

8. Scavizzi, *Controversy on Images*, 154.
9. Ibid.
10. Ugolnik, "The Libri Carolini," 23.

eventual and mounting *popular* distrust of material elements of religious devotion led to almost total reevaluation of religious materialism shortly before the time of the Reformation.[11] As examples, the work of Jean Gerson, *Expostulatio adversus corruptionem juventutis per lascivias imagenes* (1402), and the tract of Pierre d'Ailly, *De Reformatione* (1416), drew attention to the problems associated with material elements of religious devotion. However, such works from university scholars and teachers were superseded in influence by such lay religious movements as the Devotio Moderna,[12] where religious devotion begins to turn inward and away from the exuberance of material worship.

This turn, moreover, points to the fact that however much some pre-Reformation and then Protestant leaders were adamant against material worship, the objections against material components also found considerable impetus and support from the religious laity. That is, the philosophical consciousness, despite the adjective, is not the exclusive domain of intellectuals or philosophers, but can issue from the laity expressing such a mindset in equally strong fashion. Though we see in this study the frequent refrain of Reformed thinkers assigning the temptation of material worship to a simple-minded laity, the fact is that the Reformed thinkers also found sectors of the laity only too ready and willing to jettison most material worship as ill-suited for the practice of true religion. In other words, there may have been as much support among the laity for Christian "idealism" as for Christian "materialism.[13] Therefore, in this reform, one encounters the fact that reform of religious practices is not given impetus by the great Reformers alone. Popular resistance to the removal of images and the decorum is just as easily matched by a popular insistence that all be brought down. On the issue of material elements in religious devotion, it is simply not the case that while theologians write and preach, the laity merely reads and listens. Therefore, the issue of materiality in religious devotion is hardly brought

11. See, for example, Ozment, *Reformation in the Cities*, 20–44; Eire, *War*, 8–27.

12. In this movement, religious practice begins a turn from attention to the formal and material to the fervent and spiritual, and so attention to the inner life of the individual can begin to withdraw attention from the outer. But however much the statement of Thomas a Kempis that we should "Endeavor therefore to withdraw your heart from the love of visible things, and to turn yourself to things invisible" might resemble the later Reformed tradition, there are differences. While both tend to be antispeculative in theological matters, in the Reformed tradition there is a guarded hesitation to embrace fully, for example, the contention of a Kempis that "I would rather feel contrition than know the definition thereof."

13. See Pelikan, note 7.

into clearer focus by positioning the debate as one neatly but wrongly divided between intellectuals and laity. Thus, in the words of Margaret Miles, however it might be "tempting to interpret Protestant rejection of the efficacy and value of images as a result of perspectival bias of educated language users,"[14] the fact is that the issue cannot be resolved on the basis of such divisions, as the abundant disagreements between Luther and Karlstadt and Zwingli illustrate.

Thus, the philosophical consciousness presents itself both inside and outside the ranks of intellectuals. This is perhaps no better seen than in those late medieval groups deemed doctrinally deviant, such as the Cathars, Lollards, and Waldensians. Many within their ranks sloughed off virtually all "externals" as unnecessary and detrimental to the religious life. Not uncommonly, Catholic defenders of external and material components of religion noted the affinity of these heretical groups to iconoclastic sectors at the time of the Reformation. Of course, the same kind of parentage was charged to Luther and his Protestant theology at the start of the Reformation.

Andreas Bodenstein von Karlstadt

The details of the influence of Karlstadt upon the Reformed tradition are not well known, and though Reformed criticisms of material forms of religious devotion closely resemble those of Karlstadt, the historical trajectory of influence is largely unknown.[15] What is known, however, is that Karlstadt has certain ideas about religious reform and proper religious devotion that resonate with and are ultimately solidified in the practical religious reforms of the Reformed thinkers.

Andreas Karlstadt was influenced, like many of his fellow Protestant Reformers, by the spiritualism of Erasmus, and particularly by Erasmus's criticism of the externals of religion and their abuse. But whereas Luther and Erasmus eventually turned into bitter enemies, the spiritualism of Erasmus made him more congenial to the humanist trained Reformed

14. Miles, *Image*, 101.

15. Eire, in *War*, 73, contends, "Whether or not Karlstadt's iconoclastic theory had any direct effect on events in Switzerland is hard to prove." However, E. J. Furcha, editor of *The Essential Carlstadt*, 19, makes the claim that after his exile from Wittenberg and some years of wandering, Karlstadt "gained a new focus within the Reformed tradition." Christensen is correct in his *Art and the Reformation*, 36, to see in Karlstadt "the first great theorist of Reformation iconoclasm."

thinkers, even though Erasmus had as little sympathy—and probably less—for the actual measures of the Protestant Reformed tradition as he did for the Lutheran Reformation. Moreover, the Reformed Protestant Reformers were prepared to act whereas Erasmus was not, and so however much some Protestant thinkers might agree with Erasmus in his criticisms of existing religious practices, they broke with Erasmus's hesitations over implementing corrections to such practices.

However much the influence of Erasmus's critique of medieval religious devotion upon Karlstadt, especially on the point of a shared spiritualism, there are nevertheless differences between Erasmus and Karlstadt. Though Erasmus had been critical of most of the practices of medieval religious devotion, he ultimately regarded them as matters of indifference: a position not unlike that of Luther in many respects.[16] Karlstadt, however, looked upon those practices as positively evil, and ultimately, as with Zwingli, characteristic of "false religion." This is why Karlstadt and Zwingli were not slow to "enact" the framework for the practice of "true religion."

Karlstadt was Luther's senior at the University at Wittenberg and was an ardent Thomist until, in 1516, Luther challenged Karlstadt with the contention that the scholastic theologians had misunderstood both the Bible and St. Augustine. This charge greatly incensed Karlstadt who had made himself a respected scholastic theologian. Nevertheless, after many discussions and debates, Karlstadt become an Augustianian, and turned from his long study of the scholastics to Scripture and the early Church Fathers. This transition now put him in league with Luther, but only for a time. Karlstadt, as indication of his coming differences with Luther, slowly began to insist upon a great difference between the inner and the outer devotional Christian life. This was in part due to Karlstadt's exuberance over St. Augustine's *De Spiritu et Littera*, a work he declared to be "the book to be a handle and entrance to all theology."[17]

However, there was another very significant aspect of Karlstadt's thinking that would also eventually set him in opposition to Luther. Despite the Augustianian influence, Karlstadt's theology of grace was not nearly as Christologically centered as was that of Luther, nor of Staupitz—a teacher of

---

16. Luther says, for example, in his fourth sermon after Invocavit on March 12, 1522, "Therefore I must admit that images are neither here nor there, neither evil nor good, we may have them or not, as we please . . . for I cannot deny that it is possible to find someone to whom images are useful" (*Luther's Works*, Vol. 51: 86).

17. Quoted in Sider, *Andreas Bodenstein von Karlstadt*, 19.

great influence upon both Luther and Karlstadt.[18] This difference, I would suggest, is an indication that Karlstadt, largely like the Reformed thinkers, owes his reticence toward the material elements of religious devotion to a conception of God as transcendent. The Christian God as incarnate in history is a lesser consideration for them.

Karlstadt's iconoclastic spirit began to manifest itself at the time when Luther was in the Wartburg Castle. Because there was some violent destruction of images in churches, the Wittenberg reformers, headed by Karlstadt in Luther's absence, convinced the city council to proceed with a series of ordinances to have the images peacefully removed. Apparently fearful that the city council might retract the agreed upon ordinance, on 27 January 1522, Karlstadt penned the treatise "On the Removal of Images," which has the distinction of being the first significant discussion of images from the Protestant perspective, though it would be superseded by the works of Ulrich Zwingli on the same subject. As noted by Mangrum and Scavizzi, "Karlstadt thought of the pamphlet as marking the end of a successful process of renovation, but in fact it was the beginning of a long conflict which reached its conclusion in the Protestant world only fifty years later."[19]

Karlstadt in fact had published two earlier treatises, "On Holy Water and Sacred Salt" (1520) and "Instruction Concerning Vows" (1521), which portended the later treatise. In the former, Karlstadt gives voice to a classic argument of the Reformed thinkers against incorporation of materiality into a proper religious consciousness. He writes, "For this reason Christ says that true worshippers will worship God neither in Jerusalem nor upon a mountain, but only in spirit and in truth. Spirit is tied to no single place, but is in more than one place. Truth is not tied to any corporeal or visible thing; it is fastened on God alone. It does not stand in anything other than faith in God. Thus a true worshipper—the one God desires—is free and unencumbered by places and external things."[20]

Because this is a common argument for the universal as opposed to the particular presence of God—it is also found in Zwingli—the argument is of no little moment. The contention offered is that because God is omnipresent, no locality can provide greater access to God than any other "place." The sense of the universal presence of God, at least on the theoretical level, might be construed as a corollary or perhaps a push toward

---

18. Ibid.; Sider, *Karlstadt*, 44, notes that "Karlstadt's theology in 1517 and 1518 emphasized divine grace, but said little about Christ."

19. Mangrum and Scavizzi, *Reformation Debate*, 18.

20. Karlstadt, *VGU*, 94/Furcha, *The Essential Carlstadt*, 82.

the sacramentalization of the universe. This could be so simply because as the divine suffers no local confinement, but instead maintains a universal presence, the divine potentially extends to every corner of the universe. But the argument for the universal presence of God, as argued in Karlstadt and Zwingli, is not to transpose the implied restriction of local activity of God in order to expand and envelope the entire universe. Rather, the argument is to free God—but also the follower of God—from the local and particular because they limit not only God, but also the "true worshipper."

Ironically, a desacralization of the universe is set in motion with this notion of divine universal presence, simply because in this conception, the activity of God moves in the realm of spirit—mind—and not in the realm of the sensible, for the material constitutes a limitation on universal presence and divine accessibility for Karlstadt. Therefore, because our meeting place with God is not fixed in the sensible sphere, it thus remains free of the confinements of that realm. We can therefore meet with God any time, and more particularly, anywhere.

However much this argument may be thought to be derived from Christ's explication of "spirit and truth," as the Reformed thinkers often claimed, Karlstadt's conception seems rooted in metaphysical speculation of the type that the Reformed thinkers, in other contexts, decry. Perhaps the first thing noticeable is that this argument pays no attention to Luther's contention, maintained against Erasmus, of the freedom of God. The free God of Reformed Protestantism now finds his activity legislated not as a function of his freedom, but as a function of his being. Rudolf Otto, in his *Idea of the Holy*, similarly writes in consideration of and response to such a contention as that of Karlstadt:

> Does not that Sacramental idea [local presence] at once cancel itself, when thought out? Is not God "omnipresent" and "really present" always and everywhere? Such a view is often put forward, and with a confident air of assurance which is in sharp conflict with the testimony of genuine religious experience; so much so, indeed, that one is tempted to venture a very blunt reply to it. We say, then, that this doctrine of the omnipresence of God—as though by a necessity of His being He must be bound to every time and to every place, like a natural force pervading space—is a frigid invention of metaphysical speculation, entirely without religious import. Scripture knows nothing of it. Scripture knows no "Omnipresence," neither the expression nor the meaning it expresses; it knows only the God who is where He wills to be, and

> is not where He wills not to be, the *deus mobilis*, who is no mere universally extended being, but an august mystery, that comes and goes, approaches and withdraws, has its time and hour, and may be far or near in infinite degrees, "closer than breathing" to us or miles remote from us.[21]

Thus, philosophical surmises start to suspend scriptural portrayals of God. Moreover, the contention against the localized and sensible presence of God is made stronger in Karlstadt's "On the Abolition of Images," where the the chief argument against images is that material aids cannot broach a spiritual object. Added to this contention, however, is another and one deemed stronger: that all such aids are of human construction. As such, worship encompassing material elements detracts worship from its proper object—God. Only God can be a help to get to God: "You holy gluttons should mark well that God alone gives aid and no one else with him or beside him. So it must indeed be true (if the truth is to be the truth) that nothing created next to God can help us."[22] Such presumably would include not only the creations of humans, but also the creations of God—such as mountains, though Karlstadt makes reference only to the former. But the ultimate reason for opposition to any material object is that the object of worship—God—is not flesh but spirit. Here Karlstadt quotes the familiar Johannine passages. Thus no material aid to worship can begin to affect the path to a spiritual God. However, Karlstadt must address those—like Gregory the Great—who placed great value upon material images.

As mentioned earlier, most of the early Protestant Reformers were incensed over the statement and influence of Gregory the Great's dictum that images are the books of the unlearned. Karlstadt is no exception:

> Tell me, dear Gregory, or have someone else tell me, what good things could the laity learn from images? *Certainly you must say that one learns from them nothing but the life and suffering of the flesh and that they do not lead further than to the flesh. More they cannot do.* For example, from the image of the crucified Christ you learn only about the suffering of Christ in the flesh, how his head hung down and the like . . . Since, then, images are deaf and dumb, can neither see nor hear, neither learn nor teach and point to nothing other than pure and simple flesh which is of no use, it

---

21. Otto, *Idea of the Holy*, 213–14.
22. Karlstadt, *VAB*, 15/Mangrum and Scavizzi, *Karlstadt*, 29.

follows conclusively that they are of no use. But the Word of God is spiritual and alone is of use to the faithful.[23]

From the tenacious Platonism underlying these criticisms, there is one point to be noted. Karlstadt maintains that there *are* things taught by or through images, but they are the wrong things. These are things such as "how his head hung down and the like." But we can always ask why these things are not of importance, for though the Reformed thinkers largely do make their argument against material elements of religious worship rely upon the conception of God as transcendental, the particular elements informing their arguments do differ. For example, though Karlstadt's argument against any analogy between the sensible and the spiritual appears to be the main argument against images for him, he also contends, "Even if I might admit that the laity could learn something useful of salvation from images, nevertheless I could not permit that which is contrary to scriptural prohibitions and against God's will."[24] (Momentarily we shall see more indication that for Karlstadt, images do have power—even for him—but it is toward the wrong end.) Karlstadt is most emphatic that the Old Testament prohibition against images is intact. Thus, Karlstadt's essay purports to ground itself primarily in biblical injunctions. Nevertheless, one cannot describe Karlstadt's biblicism, though the heart of his attack is on images, as unmotivated by a hermeneutic of transcendence that severed spirit from matter.

In response to a traditional argument that the incarnation of Christ nullified the prohibition against images, as argued by John of Damascus in the ninth century (and also an argument used by Eck in his treatise against Karlstadt), Karlstadt reasons that however much the abrogation of ceremonial law has changed worship, it is nonetheless the case that, "Finally, you must acknowledge that Paul is a great preacher of the evangelical and New Law. He penetrated the depths of the Mosaic Law and brought it to light ... You must also say as follows: If Paul forbids images, I must flee from them ... Do you hear how evil and damaging Paul thinks images are? He says that those who praise images steal the splendour of God and offer likenesses of creatures. Therefore, Moses again and again says that God cannot tolerate our images and likenesses. Thus Paul and Moses agree."[25]

---

23. Karlstadt, *VAB*, 9/Mangrum and Scavizzi, *Karlstadt*, 24–25. (Italics mine.)
24. Karlstadt, *VAB*, 11/Mangrum and Scavizzi, *Karlstadt*, 27.
25. Karlstadt, *VAB*, 22/Mangrum and Scavizzi, *Karlstadt*, 39.

Denuded Devotion to Christ

Thus, Karlstadt depicts the message against images as ultimately unchanged from Moses to Paul insofar as the "interruption" or the interlude of the incarnated Christ is concerned. The God of Karlstadt tends to take on the character of the unchangeable and ultimately the impassible: the god of the philosophers. The incarnate Christ affects little of Karlstadt's thought on the subject of material devotion because his thought is theocentric to the degree that "Karlstadt wrote little about the activity of Christ: he always emphasized the person of Christ within the totality of God's plan of salvation. His Christ was never that inordinately concrete Lutheran Jesus *pro me,* and . . . More important for Karlstadt than the activity of Christ was the memory of Christ's sacrifice. This also influenced his Eucharistic doctrine, by negating the real presence of Christ in the sacrament."[26]

We confront in Karlstadt a phenomenon similar to that we shall see in Zwingli: a tempting love for that which they religiously and vehemently oppose. Karlstadt admits the power of images, but considers it a devilish power, though he also claims that in the last analysis, images are nothing more than their material constituents and thus not to be feared. Though attracted to images, most important perhaps is Karlstadt's love of pictures. The love of pictures however, he will juxtapose to his love of God.

> Now I want and shall say to all pious Christians that all those who stand in awe before pictures have idols in their hearts. And I want to confess my secret thoughts to the whole world with sighs and admit that I am faint-hearted and know that I ought not to stand in awe of any image and am certain that God expects of his people that they should not stand in awe of images . . . And I know that God dwelling in me is as small as my fear of idols [images] is great. For God wants to fill our whole heart and will in no way tolerate that I should have a picture before my eyes . . . And he teaches us that it is the same thing to venerate images or to be in awe of them. For this reason I should not fear any image, just as I should not venerate any. But (I lament to God) from my youth onward my heart has been trained and grown up in the veneration and worship of pictures. And a harmful fear has been bred into me from which I would gladly deliver myself and cannot. As a consequence, I stand in fear that I might not be able to burn idols.[27]

Karlstadt, of course, thought he was under scriptural mandate until such images were destroyed, but for his part in their destruction, he was

---

26. Michalski, *Reformation*, 48.
27. Karlstadt, *VAB*, 20/Mangrum and Scavizzi, *Karlstadt*, 35–36.

banished by Luther from Wittenburg.[28] Eire is correct in his contention that "The rift between Luther and Karlstadt was caused primarily by Karlstadt's reform of the cultic life of Wittenberg. Outwardly, the fundamental issues dividing the two men in 1521–1522 seem to have been issues of religious policy, not so much theology, *but inwardly their disagreement stemmed from differing interpretations of the nature of worship.*"[29]

Huldreich Zwingli

Though Calvin clearly supersedes Zwingli in prominence and influence in the Reformed tradition, both in his theological writings and also in Calvin's great Geneva political/religious experiment, it is Zwingli, nonetheless, who was the antecedent pioneer of the Reformed tradition, and thereby lent it distinctive characteristics that Calvin would bring into greater prominence. Zwingli's *Commentary on True and False Religion* (1525) has the distinction of being the earliest comprehensive treatment of Protestant theology of the Reformation, though Calvin would later follow Zwingli's work with

---

28. In 1525, Luther actually wrote a friendly preface for Karlstadt's *Apology*. Nevertheless, in his preface Luther also wrote, "In matters of doctrine, Doctor Carlstadt is my greatest antagonist and we have clashed so fiercely in these matters that all hope for reconciliation or for further dealings has been dashed." He goes on to write that "I do want to make crystal clear, however, and state that I do not endorse, nor in any way subscribe to, Carlstadt's opinion and teaching, especially with regard to the sacrament. Rather, I have written against him before and stand by that now. And I would most earnestly plead with everyone to guard against [his teaching], notwithstanding the fact that many others write on these matters in a similar manner." Quoted in Furcha, *Essential Karlstadt*, 396–97. Ozment notes in *Age of Reform*, 336–37, that "Luther's long developed aversion to 'spiritual' religion certainly influenced his position. One of his chief complaints against scholastic theologians had been that they were . . . so enamoured of the Christ who reigned in eternity that they neglected his incarnation and crucifixion in time. Karlstadt and Muntzer had appealed to the 'spiritual Christ' and accused Luther of not being able to see beyond the dead letter of Scripture and history."

29. Eire, *War*, 65–66. Sider, in *Karlstadt's Battle with Luther*, 4, contests this, claiming that "One cannot satisfactorily explain the break between Luther and Karlstadt primarily in terms of theological differences. In 1522 their disagreement was far more over strategy than over theology, and the two must not be confused." Eire, however, in *War*, 72–73, makes the following contrast between the two men concerning the Marburg Colloquy: "When Oecolampadius [a disciple of Zwingli] said [to Luther] 'don't cling so fast to Christ's humanity and flesh; raise your thoughts to Christ's divinity,' Luther responded: 'I know God only as he became human, so shall I have him in no other way' . . . For Luther and his followers, there could be no strict separation of spiritual and material . . . This is the great watershed of the Reformation." (Italics mine.)

his highly influential *Institutes of the Christian Religion*, first published in 1536. However, before Calvin's religious influence upon the city of Geneva, Zwingli would orchestrate, with scarcely any of the violence that befell Karlstadt and Luther's Wittenberg, an astonishing reconstruction of proper Christian devotion in his own Zurich that had early adopted the new Protestantism. This reconstruction followed from Zwingl's suspicion of material entities for use in religious devotion and worship. Thus, it was in Zurich after a mere two years of factionalism and public disputation, that Zwingli, by civil decree had removed all images, paintings, altars, and statuary from the church of Zurich and famously proclaimed how beautiful were the whitewashed walls.

The specifics of Zwingli's program of reform clashed as sharply with the program of Luther as had those of Karlstadt, and the inability of Luther and Zwingli at Marburg in 1529 to agree on what sense the presence of Christ in the Eucharist is to be understood, effectively divided the Reformed from the Lutheran confession. Zwingli wrote a response to Luther's treatise against the treatise of Karlstadt on images. Zwingli, however, thinks that Karlstadt's position on images—which he nevertheless supports—unnecessarily limps from the ignorance of Karlstadt.

Zwingli, unlike Luther, and as a portent of later Reformed Puritanism, insisted that there were no *adiaphora*, or indifferent matters in religious doctrine or religious practice. This of course meant that there was far less latitude in matters religious for Zwingli than Luther. This almost necessarily made Zwingli's scalpel upon religious devotional practices more severe than Luther's. This is Zwingli's basis for the radical reform measure for which Zwingli is most famously known—the prohibition of music in religious worship. For Luther, the matter of form and ceremony was a matter of indifference as long as such were not explicitly prohibited by Scripture. For Zwingli, however, there cannot be anything in religious practice that does not have the explicit sanction of Scripture. However, we will see that the fervent biblicism of Zwingli can mask the fact that Zwingli's program of religious reform is cojoined to a greater receptivity toward philosophy, despite his overt and outward denunciations of philosophy proper.

Zwingli's humanist training in part, like that of not a few of the Protestant Reformers, and similar to Karlstadt, had been significantly derived from Erasmus, and Zwingli had had a much prized correspondence with Erasmus early in his career. Zwingli himself acknowledged his debt to Erasmus, particularly on the question of material components in religious practices. However, after Zwingli turned toward concrete and practical reform of religious practice in Zurich, Erasmus, with his distaste for the actual measures of Protestant reform, broke off the correspondence with Zwingli, to Zwingli's great disappointment. By 1524, the Zwinglian reform of religion had attracted so much attention that it began to elicit response from Catholics, just as it would from Luther and the Lutherans. The Catholic Swiss cantons in and around Zurich accepted the offer of John Eck, previous and formidable debater of both Luther and Karlstadt, to defend against Zwingli and his supporters, the traditional Catholic devotional practices.

Among the chief Protestant Reformers, Zwingli is the reformer most resolute to desensualize existing religious practice. What draws even more attention to his radical program of reform is that among his fellow Protestant Reformers, Zwingli stands out as an artist, an accomplished musician, and a great lover of music. This is the case even in comparison to Luther's love of hymnody and music. But Luther does not excise these elements from religious devotion, whereas in Zwingli's reform of 1524, he bans music in religious services, a practice that stood for four centuries in the Zurich church. Moreover, in addition, he has no place for visual aids in a properly conceived religious devotion and explicitly dislikes the pictorial nature of the Catholic religious consciousness. In a manner reminiscent of Karlstadt, however, he admits that "more than other men I take pleasure in beautiful paintings and statues."[30] He also, similar to Karlstadt, writes, "Moreover, it is also wrong that the pictures teach us."[31] Thus, Zwingli, the great lover of music, accomplished musician, lover of pictures and statues, and also a poet, would reckon that these traditional accompaniments of religious devotion and worship did not belong to true religion. They must be jettisoned.

The event that set into motion Zwingli's reform of religious devotion further reveals more of the complexity of the personality of Zwingli. During August of 1519, a plague had begun to ravish Zwingli's Zurich, and though not present when the plague began, he returned to Zurich and unselfishly and daily exposed himself to the disease in faithfully performing his pastoral duties. However, in September, he himself fell prey to the plague and was rumored for dead because of the severity of his sickness. He was however restored to health, though very slowly, while the experience of the near fatal sickness became for him a defining experience of his life. In

---

30. Cited in Auksi, *Christian Plain Style*, 228.
31. Zwingli, *KCE* 89: 656/Pipkin, *Zwingli Writings*, Vol. II: 69.

the aftermath of his recovery, he composed a poem about his experience, but the words of the poem were not adequate to the voice within desiring to speak, and Zwingli turned to a musical accompaniment for his poem, entitled, "The Plague Song." This move reflects a tremendous tension and paradox in Zwingl, for in the words of his best biographer, Garside,

> Music, and music alone, could answer his desire to shape and record the immensity of the experience that he had undergone. Thus the Plague Song constitutes a natural, if not ineluctable, musical epitome of the profoundly aesthetic aspects of Zwingli's personality, just as does the fact that he chose to present the experience itself in poetic form. Yet three years later Zwingli insisted that music be prohibited completely from public worship. That so sensitive a musician and composer should make such a demand at all, not to speak of his intransigence on the subject, poses an apparent paradox which has long perplexed both his biographers and historians of music.[32]

This paradox, however, is lessened if we judge that this religious reformer who yearned for and enjoyed aesthetic elements, nevertheless bowed before a philosophical consciousness he took as more fitted to maintain religious devotion correctly than the sensual and material elements that diverted and diluted true religious devotion. In Zwingli's conception, truth must find media or vehicles capable of upholding it, but without distraction from it. The simplest way to do this is to present truth as matter of fact and not alongside nor within media capable of losing sight of its object. Therefore, one unwraps truth out of the layers that, however naturally they may express or even embody truth, are ultimately potential detractors of it and thus not servants at all, but usurpers.

However this conception may seem to juxtapose life to the life of religion to truth, this separation is but a consequence of the demarcation between true and false religion. To keep the true away from the false, moreover, it ultimately becomes necessary to pit the mind or spirit against the senses or matter. For Hegel, the muzzle of religious consciousness is its chain to the material and sensual component of human existence, while for Zwingli these components do not belong with true religion, but with false religion. For Hegel, true religion is marching toward the future with philosophical consciousness awakened; Hegel would agree with the Zwinglian assessment that Catholic material religious devotion stagnates

---

32. Garside, *Zwingli*, 26.

itself within a cumbersome religious consciousness filled with things. For Zwingli, who wants to maintain an explicitly *religious* devotion from within a philosophical consciousness, religious consciousness nevertheless begins to take on the characteristics of Hegel's philosophical consciousness, which virtually none of these reformers seem to consider, though they are highly learned individuals. One might suggest that the "paradox" spoken of by Garside and the predicament in Zwingli's thought is helpfully compared to Nietzsche's interpretation of Socrates with reference to Plato's "conversion" to philosophy. That is, Nietzsche makes allusion to the tradition that Plato became a disciple of Socrates on condition that Plato give up his poetry. Socrates, however, on his deathbed, acknowledges his rationalistic error in his request for music. Furthermore, Nietzsche identifies in the "Critique of Philosophy" as the chief error of the philosophers the flight from sensuality.[33] The difference between the two, however, is that while Socrates and Plato see themselves as launching the philosophical project, Zwingli sees himself launching a religious project in his reform of false religion.

If it is the case that Zwingli in fact embraces a philosophical consciousness, rather than a religious consciousness, what accounts for his hostility toward philosophy? To answer this question, we turn to a closer look between true and false religion in Zwingli's conception.

The comparison of true to false religion corresponds for Zwingli to a general contrast between the religion of the Protestant Reformers and that of Catholics. Zwingli portrays the difference broadly as the difference between true religion as derived from the Bible and the false religion of the Catholics as one of adherence to tradition and reason. Though the specific trait that arises out of each of these latter traits of Catholicism, according to Zwingli, is superstition and rationalism respectively, Zwingli's argument against superstition takes on its own rationalism. This is despite the fact that Zwingli is every bit the Protestant in his objection to the incorporation of philosophy into the theological task. In the following passage, he is scathing and uncompromising in his refusal to allow any epistemological role for reason or for philosophy:

> We may well call it the rash boldness of a Lucifer or a Prometheus if any one presumes to know from any other source what God is than the Spirit Himself of God. All, therefore, is sham and false

---

33. Nietzsche, *Will to Power*, 220, "Philosophers are prejudiced against appearance, change, pain, death, *the corporeal, the senses*, fate and bondage, and the aimless." (Italics mine.)

Denuded Devotion to Christ

religion that the theologians have adduced from philosophy as to what God is. If certain men have uttered certain truths on this subject, it has been from the mouth of God, who has scattered even among the heathen some seeds of the knowledge of Himself, though sparingly and darkly; otherwise they would not be true. But we, to whom God Himself has spoken through His Son and through the Holy Spirit, are to seek these things not from those who are puffed up with human wisdom, and consequently corrupted what they received pure, but from the divine oracles. For when men began to disregard these, they fell into all that is fleshly, i.e., into the inventions of philosophy, took to believing these, and, relying upon them, not only held such views as they liked about God, but forced others to hold the same.[34]

Despite this invective, one finds less of an uncompromising spirit in Zwingli toward philosophy when he steps aside from his theory of knowledge per se to criticize superstition or false religion. It is in combatting "superstition" that the reason of philosophy has some legitimacy, however much for the sake of expediency. For example, in an elucidation of his theory of "symbolic presence" of Christ in the Eucharist, Zwingli says,

> For body and spirit are such essentially different things that whichever one you take it cannot be the other. If spirit is the one that has come into question, it follows by the law of contraries that body is not; if body is the one, the hearer is sure that spirit is not. Hence, to eat bodily flesh spiritually is to assert that to be body which is spirit. I have adduced these things from the philosophers against those men who, in spite of Paul's warning to be on our guard against philosophy, Col. 2:8, have made it the mistress and instructress of the word of God, that they may see clearly how nicely they sometimes weigh their decisions and pronouncements. In short, faith does not compel sense to confess that it perceives what it does not perceive, but it draws us to the invisible and fixes all our hopes on that [cf. Heb. 11:1]. For it dwelleth not admidst the sensible and bodily, and hath nothing in common therewith.[35]

As noted by George Richards, Zwingli's attitude toward philosophy hardens when he confronts the Catholic theologians, but loosens when he greets the ancient philosophers.[36] This is generally, however, because

34. Zwingli, *VFR* 90: 643/Jackson, *True and False Religion*, 61–62.
35. Zwingli, *VFR* 90: 787/Jackson, *True and False Religion*, 214.
36. Richards, in the Introduction to Zwingli's *On True and False Religion*, 6–7: "Theoretically, at least, he is a pure biblicist. By explaining his theory of knowledge in a

Zwingli's thinking is in agreement with the philosophers who view deity as transcendent, and without reference to any material nature or entity. This is why, in Zwingli's *Commentary on True and False Religion*, he does not broach the subject of God through Christ, but rather Christ through God. This is the primary reason that the material nature and being of Christ in the incarnate Jesus in Zwingli's mind does not fundamentally affect or alter how we look upon the transcendent God—because Zwingli is presuming upon the transcendent god of the philosophers. This is also the reason that Zwingli is so unrelenting in his separation of the body from the spirit and why he writes, for example, "For I fear that if there is anywhere pernicious error in the adoration and worship of the one true God, it is in the abuse of the Eucharist."[37] Zwingli of course contends this because it was in the matter of the Eucharist that he sensed the greatest possibility of threat to the spiritual nature of God and true religion.

As mentioned earlier, it was on the point of the Eucharist that Zwingli entered into the fierce and famous debate with Luther at Marburg in 1529, where Zwingli argued that the presence of Christ in the Eucharist was symbolic and not real. The Lutheran view was always that Zwingli's position rested upon a faulty Christology. The lack of place for Christology on issues like this one as it involves materiality is a point we have already noted. Garside makes the same point: "Zwingli's rejoinder [to Luther] consists in an extended discussion of the two natures and their unity, but although he affirms the unity of Christ, he greatly emphasizes His divinity, to the point, in fact of depreciating His humanity. Such an emphasis is characteristic of Zwingli's Christology, for he always tended to stress the distinction of the two natures as against their unity, especially as the controversy with Luther over the Real Presence deepened. God is the author of Redemption, and Christ's humanity, even on the cross, plays, as it were, an auxiliary role."[38]

Because of Zwingli's view on the Eucharist, it is not a surprise that he is often seen as a protomodern: "Zwingli, however, will always be considered the forerunner of all modern Christians to whom the idea of mystery

---

prefatory section, he paves the way for his exposition of the revealed doctrine and never loses sight of the contrast between the truth of God as revealed in the Bible and 'the dreams and lies' about God taken from human reason. *He is, however, far more uncompromising in his biblicism when he meets the Catholic theologians than when he greets the ancient philosophers.*" (Italics mine.)

37. Zwingli, *VFR* 90: 774/Jackson, *True and False Religion*, 198–99.
38. Garside, *Zwingli*, 70–71.

in the Lord's Supper in a realistic and sacramental sense is offensive and who profess to worship God in spirit and in truth, that is, with an enlightened mind unhampered by baseless superstitions. For these men Zwingli will remain the Reformer of the Sixteenth Century who, in his thinking, approached most nearly to that of the modern man."[39]

Zwingli thus can hardly be conceived as an irrationalist who topples the synthesis of faith and reason of the high Middle Ages. Rather, he is continuing in that synthesis, but in a subtle fashion that may construe him, in his formal opposition to reason and philosophy, as an irrationalist. Instead, he is perhaps a harbinger on the cusp of the modern period. In a particularly trenchant and revealing remark about the sense of divine presence in the Eucharist, he reveals that his spiritualism is at one with his rationalism: "We are free from meaning to speak except with the perception of faith when we make the objection of absurdity. Nothing is absurd to faith if only you rightly understand the things that are set before faith to be believed. And if anything is absurd to faith, then it is in very truth absurd. This is the hinge on which things turn. For if I do not rightly understand the divine utterances, I shall boast in vain that I believe, or I shall teach in vain, nay dangerously, my brother to understand and believe what is not set before us as an object of belief."[40]

---

39. Richards, in the Introduction to Zwingli's *On True and False Religion*, 29. Jonathan Smith, the noted scholar of ritual, has noted in his *To Take Place*, 98–99, that "Despite what may have been the intentions of the Reformers, a new language was brought into being with respect to ritual. Rather than some rituals being 'idolatrous,' that is, false, one could speak of all rituals as being 'only' or 'merely symbolic.'" In the same pages, Smith has also drawn attention to the extraordinary significance of Zwingli's view attributed by J. P. Singh Uberoi to Zwingli's view of the Eucharist. Smith remarks that "Uberoi is part of a lengthy tradition of those both within and outside the West who identify its unique characteristics with the enterprise of (modern) science . . . Where he differs is in where he places the generating issue." He then goes on to quote Uberoi as saying: "Zwingli insisted that in the utterance 'This is my body' (*Hoc est corpus meum*) the existential word 'is' (*est*) was to be understood, not in a real, literal and corporeal sense, but only in a symbolical, historical or social sense (*significat, symbolum est or figura est*) . . . Dualism or double monism was fixed in the world-view and the life-world of the modern age, which was thereby ushered in . . . Zwingli had discovered or invented the modern concept of time in which every event was either spiritual and mental or corporeal and material but no event was or could be both at once . . . Spirit, word and sign had finally parted company for man at Marburg in 1529; and myth or ritual . . . was no longer literally *and* symbolically real or true . . . Zwingli was the chief architect of the new schism and . . . Europe and the world followed Zwingli in the event. Zwingli, the reformer of Zurich, was in his system of thought the first philosopher . . . of the modern world."

40. Zwingli, *EML* 92: 618/Furcha and Pipkin, *Zwingli Writings*, Vol. II: 242.

Zwingli's "modernism" is nicely reflected in his view that there cannot be any particular presence in the Eucharist, simply because God is everywhere. This is because as a function of God's transcendence, God is omnipresent. Zwingli writes, for example, "When, therefore I say that God is everywhere present in his essence or nature and power, I do so nor put this forth of myself (though the contemplation of the Infinite leads one rather to such a belief), but I take it from the utterances of godly men. Jeremiah 23:23–24 threatens in the words of the Lord the wicked who refused to listen to his warnings, thus: 'Am I a God at hand, and not a God afar off?'"[41]

With a distinction like this, however, Zwingli is etching toward the infinite and universal god of the philosophers, and scarcely the historical and particular God in Christ. Zwingli continues by claiming that no distinction between the local and universal presence of God can be made, "As if there were a kind different from that universal presence wherewith he is present everywhere... This, then, is my view about God's presence. As to the presence belonging to his nature, he is equally present everywhere, like the air we breathe."[42] Zwingli is here, in the words of Phillip Lee, arguing against the "sin of particularity."[43] Zwingli's view of a lack of special divine presence in the Eucharist seems prohibited by his notion of the universal presence of God. Theology is felled by rational philosophy.

Zwingli sees virtually any "externals" as threatening the sufficiency of faith: "For if faith alone be not absolutely sufficient to make blessed without the power of externals, then we fall back upon works."[44] The fact of the matter, however, is that we are thrown back upon ourselves. As I indicated in chapter 1, the irony of this position on external helps is that it should appeal most to Augustinians who regard the plight of humans as one of sole dependence upon God. The reticence expressed towards these externals, moreover, puts a huge burden upon religious devotion because one is presumed capable of nourishing the whole person on the basis of one or two human senses. This injunction seems one that for fear of error, restricts material religious devotion and favors a religious understanding that absents itself from materiality.

In Zwingli's program of reform, the abuses of worship summarily reside in erroneously thinking that a material entity can sustain a spiritual

---

41. Zwingli, *EML* 92: 587/Furcha and Pipkin, *Zwingli Writings*, Vol. II: 255.
42. Zwingli, *EML* 92: 586/Furcha and Pipkin, *Zwingli Writings*, Vol. II: 254.
43. Lee, *Against the Protestant Gnostics*, 113.
44. Zwingli, *EML* 92: 564/Furcha and Pipkin, *Zwingli Writings*, Vol. II: 239.

purpose. For Zwingli, however, there is a demarcation among religious believers concerning the desire to use material elements in religious devotion. It is the feeble of faith who need material helps for their religious devotion until "they grow up."[45] Such a contention by Zwingli seems to bear out Ozments' point, alluded to in chapter 1, that the Reformation, in attempting to raise the level of religious consciousness, in some sense was an attempt to make religious devotees into adults. Thus Zwingli can write, "It has seemed best to us . . . to prescribe as little ceremony and churchly pomp as we could . . . however, in order to keep the act from being completely dull and bare and also to make some allowance for human weakness, we have—as here specified—prescribed for the act what ceremonies which we . . . thought useful and apt."[46]

In this remarkable passage, the presumption seems to be that religious devotion that is "completely dull and bare" is actually not so to the strong, but only to the weak. The weak must be enticed by a husk, without which they are not drawn to the kernel, whereas the truly devout will readily discard the outer for the inner. This is as it should be in Zwingli's mind because the focus of religious devotion is the mind, shorn of the senses and thus anything that tickles the senses is suspect. Therefore, coupled with the transcendental and universally present God is the human who rises above material and sensual encumbrances. In Zwingli human anthropology is desensualized in the interest of a attaining a transcendent Truth, as shorn of the material as possible.

Thus, ceremony and pomp are detractors for Zwingli because truth is unaided by either. The notion of "naked truth" is prominent in the Reformed tradition as an emphasis upon a truth unencumbered by unnecessary layers. Zwingli's program of reform is one in which he attempts to channel religious devotion into an engagement of the mind virtually bereft of benefit from the senses. He writes that "faith . . . is utterly unrelated to anything involving sensation,"[47] and he comments upon the endlessly repeated verse about "spirit and truth" that "those who worship him can or should do so in no more just a manner than by consecrating their mind

---

45. Zwingli, *CME* 89: 605. Of course Zwingli is not the only religious leader to share this viewpoint, nor is it confined just to Protestants. It is common among other apologists for "naked truth."

46. Zwingli, *ABN* 92: 14.

47. Zwingli, *VFR* 90: 798/Jackson and Heller, *Zwingli's Commentary on True and False Religion*, 126.

to him."[48] Part of the reason that there is in the Zwinglian reform an "unequalled excision of sensuous impediments"[49] is that the senses not only confine the individual worshipper, but they also confine God. Thus, sensual and material forms of worship intimate that God is here and thus "bind God to a place and to time."[50] Therefore, inasmuch as human persons are bound by such things, they must break the bounds of such things so as to partake of the company of God, and this takes place in the mind.[51] It is not, therefore, unnatural that this conception would place a premium upon religious knowledge or understanding, and conversely, pay particular attention to avoidance of error.

John Calvin

John Calvin stands as the most influential religious thinker of the Reformed tradition, though some have contended, like Ozment, that Calvin "was the least original of the major reformers."[52] The influence of Calvin upon the Reformed tradition in great part stems from the magnificence of his theological acumen in the *Institutes of the Christian Religion*, but in addition from his administration of religious life in Geneva. Calvin's theological work went through five editions, and the last one, of 1559, has virtually the same standing among Protestants as Thomas' *Summa Theologica* has among Catholics.

Like his fellow Protestant Reformers, Calvin exhibits a general hostility toward philosophy. Somewhat as in Zwingli, however, we find in Calvin

---

48. Zwingli, *VFR* 90: 853/Jackson and Heller, *Zwingli's Commentary on True and False Religion*, 248.

49. Auksi, "Simplicity and Silence," 345.

50. Zwingli, *Auslegung des 25. Artikels* 89: 248/Furcha and Pipkin, *Zwingli Writings*, Vol. I: 173.

51. Bouyer, *Christian Spirituality*, 78, comments regarding the mindset of Zwingli that "It is important that we should study this state of mind, as it contributed to forming average Protestantism much more than did Lutheranism . . . We can describe their [Zwinglian and Reformed] mentality historically by saying that it was a radical, and above all a rationalizing, form of those 'evangelical' tendencies to be found among the intellectual bourgeoisie on the eve of Luther's Reformation and influenced to a greater or lesser degree by Erasmus." Lee, in *Against*, 57, writes of Luther: "The solid earthiness of his personality militated against a spiritualizing theology."

52. Ozment, *Age of Reform*, 372. Michalski, *Reformation*, writes that "Calvin's theological system was perhaps less original and differentiated than Luther's, but it was more cohesive."

Denuded Devotion to Christ

elements of his thought indicating some presence of the philosophical consciousness.[53] As example, and like Zwingli, Calvin most often argues against material worship from the perspective of the presumed incompatibility of that worship with God as transcendent. For Luther, however, the retreat to God as transcendent is a retreat from the "visibility" of God as evidenced and seen in the passion and cross of Christ.

In sum, Calvin seems to restrict the visibility of God by reference to the distinctive majesty and glory of God. Thus Calvin writes that, "We are similar to God only in our souls, and no image can represent him. That is why people who try to represent the essence of God are madmen. For even their souls of little worth cannot be represented. God is spirit—says the Scripture—and yet they want to give him a body . . . Since God has no similarity to those shapes by means of which people attempt to represent him, then all attempts to depict him are an impudent affront . . . to his majesty and glory."[54]

Lest however we think that the material incarnation of Christ would modify this assessment, Calvin remarks in his *An Inventory of Relics* concerning Christ, that

> All admit, without dispute, that God carried away the body of Moses from human sight, lest the Jewish nation should fall into the abuse of worshipping it. What was done in the case of one ought to be extended to all, since the reason equally applies. But not to speak of saints, let us see what Paul says of Christ himself. He declares, that after the resurrection of Christ he knew him no more after the flesh, intimating by these words, that every thing carnal which belonged to Christ should be consigned to oblivion and discarded, in order that we may make it our whole study and endeavour to seek and possess him in spirit.[55]

---

53. It has been contended by Partee, *Calvin and Classical Philosophy*, 51, that "Calvin's view of man is perhaps more indebted to the insights of the philosophers than any other area of his thought." Coupled with this contention is the admission by the Reformed scholar Dewey Hoitniga that "It is remarkable that, in addition to Scripture, Calvin turns to confirmation of his main doctrines about the knowledge of God in the opening chapters of the *Institutes* not to the fathers but to the writings of classical pagan authors, especially Plato and Cicero." Hoitenga, "Faith and Reason in Calvin's Doctrine of the Knowledge of God," 23.

54. Calvin, *SR* 54: 149.

55. Calvin, *IR* 34: 410/Beveridge, *Tracts and Treatises*, Vol. I: 290.

In Calvin's mind, there are two reasons, working on opposite poles, that militate against material aids in religious devotion: one that concerns God and one that concerns us. The first appears to concern the nature of God inasmuch as it is a nature which in principle defies depiction, but the fact is that it is not the *nature* of God that is problematic for material depiction, but instead the *nature of soul or spirit*, whether divine or human. To see this, we can ask if the difficulty would be overcome if God had a body. However, we are prevented from answering this question directly because the second quotation rules out the value of any body, even that of Christ, as buttressed by the interpretation of the text from the Apostle. Here we encounter the overarching reason for the reticence toward images that flows from Calvin's contention that "What was done in the case of one ought to be extended to all, since the reason equally applies." In short, even with Christ as example, the larger point does not change, and that point is that humans are only too prone to pursue material elements for religious devotion. But this contention merely throws us back on the question of whether this propensity is to be faulted. Moreover, from the fact that Calvin's contention sees nothing different in the case of Christ than that of Moses, nor in the case of material depiction of spirit, whether human or divine, Calvin's argument would seem then to deny wholesale the value of material elements in religious devotion.

Ann Kibbey claims that "Calvin's theory of visual art is that of a materialist who fears that he can think no further than he physically sees."[56] This seems to me to be substantially correct. Wilkins concurs: "Calvin's thought on this point sheds light on a feature of his aesthetics: Calvin assumes that art represents the sensible."[57] If this is an accurate assessment of Calvin's view, then Calvin, like Karlstadt and Zwingli, seems doubtful of the connection between the material and the spiritual. Because Luther affirms the connection, he can say "I suppose there is nobody, or certainly very few, who do not understand that yonder crucifix is not my God, for my God is in heaven, but that this is simply a sign."[58] For Luther, moreover, misuse does not have the power to nullify proper use. Thus, Luther argues that

> Now, although it is true and no one can deny that the images are
> evil because they are abused, nevertheless we must not on that

---

56. Kibbey, *Interpretation*, 46–47.

57. Willis-Watkins, "Reform," 48.

58. Luther, "The Fourth Sermon after Invocavit," March 12, 1522, in *Luther's Works*, Vol. 51: 84.

account reject them, nor condemn anything because it is abused. This would result in utter confusion. God has commanded us in Deut. 4[:19] not to lift up our eyes to the sun [and the moon and the stars], etc., that we may not worship them, for they are created to serve all nations. But there are many people who worship the sun and the stars. Therefore we propose to rush in and pull the sun and stars from the skies. No, we had better let it be. Again, wine and women bring many a man to misery and make a fool of him [Ecclus. 19:2; 31:30]; so we kill all the women and pour out all the wine. Again, gold and silver cause much evil, so we condemn them. Indeed, if we want to drive away our worst enemy, the one who does us the most harm, we shall have to kill ourselves, for we have no greater enemy than our own heart, . . . And so on—what would we not do?[59]

Certainly part of the difference on this issue concerns the fear of error and the differing degrees of anxiety with which the Reformed thinkers approach it, in contrast to Luther and the Catholic tradition. In the case of the image, possibility of error is eliminated if the image is eliminated. In Calvin, this move is plausible to make, but not for Luther. Nevertheless, to make such a move narrows the domain of religious devotion because to lessen error, one must narrow the possibilities for error to occur. The concept of naked truth already marks out the narrow anthropological path for a religious devotion faithful to true religion, but greater caution toward error narrows the path even more. Thus, much of the Reformed tradition is willing to subdue or ignore a huge amount of human sensibility which it cast aside as the cost of guarding truth. Ozment, in describing this phenomenon in Protestantism writes, "It would rather have a little than risk a lot . . . because it needs simplicity and truth."[60]

---

59. Ibid., 85.

60. Ozment, *Protestantism*, 54. This move comes with a price: Evelyn Underhill, *Worship*, 21, contends that "exclusion of the sensible is such that it could never serve the religious needs of a creature poised between the worlds of spirit and sense, and participating in both." John Dillenberger has commented, "Protagonists for the spirit usually assume that its virtue is self-evident, and they are hardly aware that the subtle sins of the spirit are as devastating, sometimes more so, than those of the body," "Visual Arts as Paradigm," 234. By contrast Thomas O'Meara, "The Aesthetic Dimension in Theology," 206, has written, "The Roman Catholic personality and vision does not rest easily in verbal expressions," while at the same time admitting the fear of Protestants that "it aims at sacramental transparence to the divine but sometimes reaches only one or another form of idolatry."

The juxtaposition between spirit or mind and materiality restricts immensely Calvin's otherwise lush sense of God's gracious accommodation to the human condition. God reveals Himself as the true God in Calvin's thought by his capacity to present Himself for our human experience. This notion, however, is difficult to reconcile with his depiction of the transcendent and not particularly immanent presence of God in the sensual world. Divine transcendence and divine accommodation are in tension: the vehicles of permitted mediation between God and persons in Calvin seem to align themselves to a Western philosophical consciousness where the "mind's eye" of intellectual discernment severs understanding from much, short of disembodied intellection. Speaking of Calvin on this point, David Willis-Watkins has written,

> It is a curious thing that Calvin does not bring to bear on his treatment of images what he uses constructively elsewhere in his theology—his view that God creates what delights us, not just what is useful for us . . . Calvin does not seem to extend the argument—about God's also creating for our delight—when it comes to any images in worship . . . Calvin apparently has no experience (either personally validated or acknowledged charitably in others) of an image (of Christ or a cross or of a depiction of saints' faithful witnessing) being an instrument by which sinners are convicted, the love of God manifested, and believers instructed in the way they are to live.[61]

According to Calvin, while the knowledge of God provides man with knowledge of himself, the knowledge of God is ultimately only possible—because of human limitations—because God accommodates himself in revelation to those human limitations. Calvin, however, heightens the pedagogical purpose of divine revelation by seeing it as indicating the huge gap in the chain of being between God and humans, but also to indicate the goodness of God in bridging that gap, i.e., accommodation. As has been noted by Calvin scholars, the principle of accommodation has "far-reaching ramifications and effects in his hermeneutics and thus for what he accepts *as true doctrine*. It provides a way of distinguishing between proper and improper language, between what can be said properly of God and what is only a matter of expression. It makes it possible, for instance, to criticize passages that speak of the repentance of God in the light of the

---

61. Willis-Watkins, "Reform," 48–50.

Denuded Devotion to Christ

alleged immutability of God. It is particularly here that Calvin's thought has become under attack in contemporary theology. (Italics mine.)"[62]

Calvin's conception of a transcendental God fuels his argument against images and reveals a resistance stemming from a too easy identification with the god of the philosophers. That is, the manner in which Calvin's lush sense and use of the principle of accommodation is alternatively used and resisted, further reveals evidence that his reticence against material elements of devotion stems from the resistance toward materiality by the philosophical consciousness. That is, in Calvin accommodation cannot accommodate images, but accommodation legitimizes Scripture in ascribing human characteristics to God. Moreover, on this latter point, the Reformed tradition may come close to conceiving of God as impassible. The remarks of Pelikan here are helpful for indicating how the conceptual god of the philosophers infiltrates thinkers claiming to keep their God away from philosophy.

> The other Christian doctrine whose development was significantly affected by the continuing dominance of Greek thought was the doctrine of God. Implicit in the biblical view of God as the Creator was the affirmation of his sovereign independence: God was not dependent on his creatures as they were on him. But in their assertion of the freedom of God, the prophets emphasised at the same time his involvement with the covenant people in love and wrath. Therefore the Old Testament doctrine of the sovereign freedom of God could not be synonymous with the philosophical doctrine of divine impassibility . . . It is significant that Christian theologians customarily set down the doctrine of the impassibility of God as an axiom, without bothering to provide very much biblical support or theological proof . . . Nevertheless, any such concept had to be squared with the assertions of both the Old and the New Testament that God was wrathful against sin, as well as with the confession that Christ the crucified was divine. Some Christian theologians went so far as simply to identify the Christian doctrine of God with the philosophical rejection of anthropomorphism.[63]

With the last point made by Pelikan, one can consider the contention made by Halbertal and Margalit that "The central effort of philosophical religion is the attempt to attain a proper metaphysical conception of God. This conception not only is a necessary condition for the worship of God

---

62. Van der Kooi, "Within Proper Limits," 371.
63. Pelikan, *Emergence*, 52–53.

but also constitutes the high point of religious life. Philosophical religion, which attempts to purify the divinity from anthropomorphism, considers the crux of the problem of idolatry to be the problem of error."[64]

A kind of intellectualism thus naturally appears among thinkers, like the Reformed thinkers, who retract the physical into the metaphysical. The fear of anthropomorphism in the Reformed conception, however, is not ultimately due to a desire to separate God from humans, however much religious devotion in this tradition may have to make its way off the familiar tracks of matter.

---

64. Halbertal and Margalit, *Idolatry*, 71.

3

Protestantism and Rationalism

Aligning Early Protestants with Rationalism

When reading early sixteenth century Protestant Reformers, one easily forms the impression that making religion purer or the striving for "true religion" meant minimizing or even eradicating any place for material elements in religious devotion. Referencing the issue of icons, Ambrosios Giakalis judges the Reformation attempt to expunge religious practice of matter, a dubious move to religion constructed upon uneasy philosophical rocks. He writes, "It is not certain whether the iconoclasts were always conscious of what they were aiming at, or of their less immediate motives. The combating of idolatry through the rejection of icons was a manifest and conscious rejection of Hellenism. The complete rejection of matter, however, in the name of a spiritual worship, was inescapably a return to Neoplatonism. As regards the former, the rejection was conscious. As regards the latter, was there not even the smallest suspicion of a return?"[1]

Characteristic of thinkers like Karlstadt, Zwingli, and Calvin are emphases upon a spiritual understanding that undermines the place and value of material devotional aids. The Reformed opposition to the use and value of the material elements of religious devotion is not unique to the early Reformed tradition, but characteristic to some extent of many Protestant traditions emerging at the time of the Reformation and of earlier reform movements such as that found among the Cathars and Lollards. The early Reformed thinkers articulated their opposition to material aids, however, with a rigor and intensity unmatched by few other Protestant confessions. Certainly the response from Catholic thinkers to the question of

---

1. Giakalis, *Images*, 116–17.

appropriate media for religious devotion is calculated chiefly as response to the Reformed position. Cardinal Bellarmine, for example, in his major work *Controversies*, published from 1586 to 1596, by far opposes the views of Calvin more than any other Protestant on this question.[2]

Iconoclasm brought to debate the issue of the appropriateness of material visual aids in religious devotion early in the Reformation and had the effect of dividing Protestant from Protestant and particularly Lutheran from Reformed. Though Luther would break with Karlstadt and ban him from Wittenberg for his apparent encouragement of the iconoclastic destruction in that city, Luther's response of defending images is sometimes interpreted as prompted by Luther's fear of a Reformation proceeding too fast, rather than from any actual conviction of the value of images in devotional practice. Nevertheless, on the issue of images, Luther would argue that Karlstadt's opposition was indicative of rationalism present in the despisers of such religious aids.

The Reformed position eventually found itself opposing both Lutherans and Catholics on the use of material aids in religious devotion, and the controversy is rightly seen by some historians of the Reformation as the first significant issue dividing the early Protestants.[3] Though certainly not the strongest advocate of such religious aids, Luther's position nonetheless soon met with hostility from Reformed thinkers who regarded such a position as exemplifying the "unfinished" Lutheran Reformation. Out of deference to the great respect in which they otherwise held Luther, moreover, early Reformed thinkers refrained from specific attacks on him in their attacks on the use of images and art in religious devotion. But as the Reformation propelled itself into succeeding generations, Luther was often openly held in contempt for his position by later Reformed thinkers.[4]

Though some hostility to things physical as unfit vehicles for truth is expressed in the rise of Western philosophy as classically expressed in the thought of Plato and Neo-Platonists, antipathy has most often developed in the Western world from within explicitly religious traditions, and it is in these traditions that we most often infer its ultimate origins. However, to frame the question of the relation of a religious tradition, intent on religious

---

2. Bellarmine, Robert, *Disputationes de Controversiis Christianae Fidei*, 1599.

3. For example, Eire, *War*, 2.

4. John Foxe, the English author of the famous *Foxe's Book of Martyrs*, 348, notes that because of Luther's support of images in England, people "give clean over the reading of Luther, and fall almost in utter contempt of his books."

reform, to a philosophical tradition expressing reservations over the place of physical things in the realm of the spiritual, we encounter the ironic fact that typically the same religious traditions desiring distance from images and art as a part of the reform of religion, like the early Reformed tradition, also desire distance from philosophy, also like the early Reformed tradition. Moreover, the opposition to art and to philosophy were at least partially exhibited by most emerging Protestant groups at the time of the Reformation. This religious opposition to both reflects in part the trademark Protestant concern for a true or right belief that is suspicious of making the work of the artist or the philosopher not only a source or vehicle of truth, but perhaps of giving them a *religious* voice at all.

The question of proper theological sources and appropriate vehicles by and in which to convey Christian truth are of pressing concern at the time of the Reformation, with the luxurious sources and vehicles in Catholicism—to include the ritual and images and art strong in Catholic tradition—perceived as its frailty by many Protestants. The Reformed tradition, moreover, presents some of the strongest Protestant protests against material aids in religious practice. The question of the conceptual link between such a reforming religious tradition and philosophical rationalism also confronts the added fact that in Catholicism the tie with philosophy as philosophy is largely acknowledged, encouraged, and cultivated, and yet images, art, and ritual survive and in fact proliferate.

At this juncture one can raise the obvious point that a difference between Catholicism and Reformed Protestantism on this issue can only be clarified by reference to the particular philosophy undergirding the respective acceptance or suspicion of material accompaniments in religious devotion. Thus, it is customary to see in the strong Augustinian character of Protestant theology and anthropology resonances with a Platonism resisting the sacramentalism underpinning much of the use of material aids in religious devotion.[5] The early Reformed reticence toward the use of the

---

5. As example, Gilson, *Christianity and Philosophy*, particularly chapter 2, "Calvinism and Philosophy." Margaret Miles, however, sees a change in Augustine toward the material element of religious devotion in her *Fullness of Life*, 80: "In his early work, *De Vera Religione*, he said that miracles no longer occurred as they had in the early church because they were necessary only in a time when people needed instant dramatizations of the efficacy of Christian faith. Now that people can *reason* to Christian faith, miracles are no longer required. But by the time, toward the end of his life, that he wrote Book XXII of the *City of God*, Augustine was collecting, verifying, and publishing accounts of miracles as the sign of God's direct activity in the concrete world of events and bodies. Augustine's interest in miracles is not a concession to popular credulity but rather

material in religious devotion, however, advances a kind of basic rational religion—and thus is not simply spiritualism disciplining itself against the material excesses of Christian devotion.[6] As such, there is a mounting historical and cultural shift toward secular modernity implied in the Reformed penchant for rationalism as a Protestant principle, though with the unintended consequence of advancing toward secular modernity.

Historically in the West, the religionist or mythologist and the philosopher have been frequently on uneasy terms. Perhaps at no time was there a greater attempt to formally separate philosophy from religion than at the time of the Protestant Reformation; nonetheless, the question posed is, Was the Reformed religious attempt to minimize or eradicate the role of the material element in religion actually a shift that undermines, a least in part, the goal of true religion?[7]

We can see that material elements that previously accounted for much of the religious life start to ebb, as the religious consciousness increasingly gives way to the desensualized spiritual idea that exemplifies philosophical consciousness. The rationalism explicit in philosophical consciousness is present in the Reformed tradition by the minimizing of materiality from the focus of religious consciousness, and in that transition, the Reformed tradition begins to compromise itself as a *religious* tradition.[8] Specifically,

---

the wave of the future, in which both educated and uneducated people would share the excitement of evidences of God's power in the sensible world." I think part of the reason for the shift in Augustine on this point is his decreasing sympathy with philosophy in his later life. As a convert to Christianity from pagan philosophy, he had naturally adopted the "hierarchical view" described by Miles, 108, but with a change: "The identification of God with the material objects of devotion represents a shortcut not permitted the hierarchical view. The concern of the iconoclasts was precisely the loss of the hierarch to material objects."

6. The correlation of the Reformed tradition with philosophy takes place in the scholarly literature at the level of identifying either individual Reformed thinkers with particular philosophical influences, or the Reformed tradition with specific schools of philosophy. Fueling any such identifications are the strong Reformed emphases on the transcendence of God and the necessity of internal or "spiritual" religion. Understandably, such emphases have sometimes brought the various charges of Platonism, Gnosticism, and severe dualism to this tradition. A weightier charge on occasion has been that Reformed thought depicts God as the god of the philosophers.

7. Ugolnik, "The Libri Carolini," 23, makes some attempt to connect the iconoclastic mentality with "distinctly Western religious and critical consciousness." Ugolnik's article, however, deals almost exclusively with the traditional argument of Eastern and Western Christianity over the word versus the image.

8. No study known to me argues that the Reformed Protestant tradition as it originates with Zwingli, Calvin, and Karlstadt takes on a shift of consciousness in its suspicion

the resonances of the rationalism implicit in philosophical consciousness take place on three levels in Reformed religion: (1) in metaphysics, where spirit and truth desensualize metaphysics—and where the tendency now becomes strong to view God as increasingly transcendent, though not spiritually distant; (2) in a desensualized epistemology—where the intellect is pitted against the senses, and the word is pitted against the image; (3) and in a desensualized anthropology—where the exaltation of cognitive understanding marginalizes the affective dimension that material devotional aids had nourished.

The reticence of the Reformed tradition toward the religious value of materiality is not fully understood through an alignment of that tradition with particular philosophical doctrines, such as Platonism. Rather, this transition is more significantly a broad historical transition from "religious" to "philosophical" consciousness, where the association of materiality to religion and religious practice becomes increasingly viewed as primitive or superstitious or simply, simple-minded. The negative judgment upon the propriety of the material components for religious devotion represents a conceptual shift in religious practice that can be identified in its particulars as a shift of anthropological and historical consciousness.[9]

Antipathy of Reformation Religion for Philosophy

The effort to connect a Protestant reform of material religious practices with a conceptual consciousness has been partly neglected because early Protestant religion is in overt opposition to philosophy proper and thus seems removed from the acids of too much infectious rationalism. Thus, before addressing more specifically the compatibility of the Reformed tradition with a philosophical consciousness, we must briefly characterize

---

toward the material elements of religion. There are, however, many studies analyzing the fact that Protestant religious reform altered a prior religious sensibility given to images, relics, pilgrimages, and a host of other material religious objects and practices. Absent from these studies, however, is any sustained argument to see in the devaluation of the material components in "true religion," emergence of a consciousness that can be described as philosophical.

9. Halbertal and Margalit, *Idolatry*, 2, contend, "The central effort of philosophical religion is the attempt to attain a proper metaphysical conception of God. This conception not only is a necessary condition for the worship of God but also constitutes the high point of religious life. Philosophical religion, which attempts to purify the divinity from anthropomorphism, considers the crux of the problem of idolatry to be the problem of error."

the sources of the general Protestant antagonism toward the philosophical enterprise. In making the claim to find a philosophical consciousness in Reformed Protestantism, one must confront the fact that in early Protestantism, neither Lutheran nor Reformed religion is known for its affinity for philosophy. Scrutinizing this relationship will clarify somewhat the nature of the hostility between the early Reformers and philosophy.

The early Protestant Reformers saw a gulf between faith and reason that was often expressed in hostility toward philosophy and speculation. However, ultimately these latter characteristics were derived from the former, and they, from theological contentions. Furthermore, the gulf between faith and reason is a consequence of the distance and disparity conceived by the Reformers to exist between God and humans. Ozment has described a shift at the time of the Reformation that will have consequences for the Reformers' attitude toward philosophy:

> Here Luther contradicted the most basic of all medieval axioms: the belief that likeness to God was the indispensable condition of both saving knowledge of him and a saving relationship with him. In medieval theology, like could only truly know like. This was the underlying rationale of monastic practices: through rigorous physical and intellectual exercises to replace one's own false self with a godlike self. It was the precondition of mystical union: "Our becoming like God [*similitudo*]," wrote Gerson, "is the cause of our union with him." And it was the raison d'etre of the sacramental system of the church: infused grace qualitatively conforms human to divine being. The final goal of monk, mystic, and pilgrim alike was conformity so complete that only God remained an object of consciousness, a point where likeness gave way to identity. Medieval theology remained devoted to the proposition that God became man so that men could be godlike. For the medieval theologian the central religious concept was accordingly *caritas*-love-not faith. The way of salvation was *fides caritate formata*, faith formed by acts of love. Faith alone, by contrast, was only an initial intellectual assent to the data of revelation made by one who was still far from pure and godly.[10]

Because of this Protestant understanding of the divine-human relation, "unlikeness" would become one unitive principle in Protestant religion. This would present a different conception of reconciliation to God than in medieval Catholicism. In Protestant thought, to begin to close the

---

10. Ozment, *Age of Reform*, 241–42.

Denuded Devotion to Christ

distance to God meant to realize the distance from God. This realization of separation was incumbent in the despair of the monk Luther, and whence his statement, "Therefore I did not love a just and angry God, but rather hated and murmured against him."[11] Acceptance by God for Luther seemed precluded by the distance from God unceasingly fed by human sinfulness. But cognizant of the distance, and despairing of the effort to close it, Luther conceived the idea that the "righteousness of God" explicitly referenced in St. Paul meant that God himself in Christ had bridged the distance created and sustained by human sin. What remained for sinners was acceptance of Christ's sacrifice for their sins, and gratitude that He had done something out of love for them that even saintly sinners could not do for themselves. Thus, sinners were identified with God *sola fide*, and not by their own works of love. God had identified Himself with persons in His sacrifice for their sins, rather than humans purging themselves of their sin so as to be identified with God. In this manner belief in the efficaciousness of Christ's deed comes to achieve prominence in Protestant thinking and replaces love as the hallmark of religious thought that it had been in Catholic thought because "to be conformed with God meant to agree with his judgment that all men are sinful and still believe his promise to save them nonetheless."[12]

Putting faith and belief into prominence, coupled with the Protestant principle of "unlikeness," has ramifications that extend beyond the salvific question of justification before God, to the much-debated medieval question of the relation of faith to reason. The principle of unlikeness between God and humans now accentuates the difference between the revelation that comes from God and the reason that issues from humans. The question of proper and reliable theological sources is thus framed for these Reformers: *sola biblia*. The majority of early Protestant Reformers therefore seek to remove philosophy from faith because the medieval project of attempting to fuse faith and reason depended upon the sense of likeness that the Reformers rejected. This sense of unlikeness undermined the viability and efficacy of a human enterprise like philosophy that presumed to proceed as if it could explain the things of God without the assistance of God. Calvin, though not as hostile to philosophy as Luther, in part because of Calvin's humanist education, nonetheless maximally constrains the viability of philosophy for the theological task by making a distinction between

11. Bainton, *Here I Stand*, 49.

12. Ozment, *Age of Reform*, 243. In the same work, 316, Ozment quotes Sebastian Castellio as complaining, "The Calvinists want men to be judged not on the basis of their morals, but according to their beliefs."

one kind of understanding of earthly things; another of heavenly. I call "earthly things" those which do not pertain to God or his Kingdom, to true justice, or to the blessedness of the future life; but which have their significance and relationship with regard to the present life and are, in a sense, confined within its bounds. I call "heavenly things" the pure knowledge of God, the nature of true righteousness, and the mysteries of the Heavenly Kingdom. The first class includes government, household management, all mechanical skills, and the liberal arts. In the second are the knowledge of God and of his will, and the rule by which we conform our lives to it.[13]

The Reformers seemed to have also derived from the Franciscan medievalist William of Ockham (c.1287–1349) something of the idea of the radical freedom of God. This notion achieves much the same effect as the principle of unlikeness between God and humans. In Ockham's theology, emphasis upon the freedom of God functions to remove the philosophical constraints fastened upon God by theologians indebted more to the parameters of philosophy than to recognition of the freedom of God. Therefore, in this conception, God, being free, commands His will to be done. But the identification of God with the transcendentals—the good and the beautiful—now seems tenuous if the true shall only be defined by itself and without reference to anything else. As noted by Ozment, this consequence shifted the ethical anxiety of the Protestant in a direction different from that inherited in Catholicism:

> In the classic Protestant traditions, both Lutheran and Reformed, as distinct from the reigning Thomist tradition of the late Middle Ages, God's freedom and sovereignty were seen to transcend his goodness and love, though Protestants believed that the latter were also very real . . . Such a perspective on religion with roots in late medieval Augustianism and Ockhamism, made the nature of God a far more burning question for Protestants than the quality of an individual's moral life.[14]

13. *ICR* 32: 313–14/Beveridge, *Institutes*, Book II: 234.

14. Ozment, *Protestantism*, 198–99. On this very point, the Reformed tradition manages to maintain, if not in fact escalate, the traditional ethical emphases found in Catholic religion. For this reason, Ozment questions whether Calvinists were really Protestants. In his *Age of Reform*, 379, he writes: "For Calvin, good works did not have the direct bearing on salvation that medieval theology taught; they attested divine favor and gave presumptive evidence of election, but they did not put one in a position to expect salvation as condign merit. On the other hand, Calvin's teaching, like his conduct of the Genevan church, once again made good works and moral behavior the center of religious life and

Predictably then, in the famous debate between Luther and Erasmus, Erasmus, who was impatient with Luther's desire to pin down fine theological points, does nonetheless insist that "God must be good." Luther's reply is telling for the Catholic-Protestant difference: he contended, "Let God be God."[15] But letting God be God makes the assimilation of faith to reason uneasy simply because if the identity of God is congruous only with God, then there is hardly room for the interface between faith and reason, much less ethics or aesthetics. Such theological ideas make the Erasmian Catholic tradition nervous, as it had with some of the intervening medieval Christian tradition of philosophy that both Luther and Calvin would now oppose.

Roots of the Philosophical Consciousness within Protestant Religion

It may seem surprising to find Calvin making frequent reference to "Christian philosophy," a term in use by various Christian thinkers in both the classical and medieval period, but given particular prominence by Erasmus.[16] Like Erasmus, Calvin means by the term the wisdom of a true Christian piety. The term has no reference to any effort at a synthesis of philosophy and Christianity in the medieval sense of the attempt of faith seeking understanding, nor of the reconciliation of faith and reason. The link between "Christian philosophy" and philosophy proper seems severed. The

---

reintroduced religious anxiety over them. In Calvinism the presence or absence of good works came to be taken as a commentary on one's eternal destiny." Further contrasts between the Lutheran and Reformed tradition on the resulting ethical difference can be seen in Luther's reticence to use the Law in the Christian life, but willingness to use art, whereas Calvin will use the Law, but not art. Analogously, the comparatively lesser ethical emphases of Lutheranism in relation to the Reformed tradition seem to further distance the two traditions. Perhaps one could conjecture in response to Ozment's point, that the transcending of God's love and goodness by his freedom and sovereignty—beliefs common in Protestantism—perhaps finds some analogy, however loose, in later modern science, where the separation of truth from ethics became the hallmark of a universe indifferent toward humans. It is noteworthy that Perry Miller, in his masterful though now dated study of the American Jonathan Edwards, claims that the Calvinist Edwards made way for "America's sudden leap into modernity" by way of a Calvinist theology which made God appear indifferent to humans, similar to the way that science would later make the universe appear indifferent toward humans.

15. Luther, "On the Bondage of the Will," 259.

16. See the Ford Lewis Battles translation of Calvin's *Institutes*, 7–8, for a brief but good overview of the history of this term.

Protestantism and Rationalism

Catholic Erasmus and the Protestant Calvin appear to agree that they shall do philosophy from theology. In addition, when both come to a conception of proper Christian philosophy, their ideas are substantially in agreement. They show a suspicion of attention to the "externals" of religious life, and they affirm that the profusion of Catholic devotional practices had misplaced Christ. These criticisms of medieval religious life often have as their corollary the emphasis upon the necessity and importance of inner rather than outer religion. Thus, emphasis in this conception is upon the fervent rather than the formal, while the true image of Christ is in the imitation of Christ, rather than the adoring and contemplative gaze fastened onto the image, for example. The resulting form of religious life and devotion thus moves away from the formal and toward the ethical in both Erasmus and Calvin.

Not only is it the case that Christian philosophy for Erasmus and Calvin is not about the assimilation of Christianity to philosophy, but Christian philosophy is characterized by a deliberate distinction between Christianity and philosophy, and the added attempt, particularly by Erasmus, to portray the quibbling of the philosophers as so much unnecessary and spurious nonsense. Calvin's split between the divine revelation undergirding theology and the human reason responsible for philosophy appears to give him leave also of the philosophers on the subject of religion.

However, the early Reformed tradition gave ear to philosophy in more subtle fashion. This occurs in their embrace of the rationalism of the philosophical consciousness which is rejected by Luther. In other words, Luther's rejection of philosophy is a rejection of rationalism; the Reformed thinker's criticism of philosophy must be read carefully because it reveals significant retention of rationalism most evident in their criticism of material religion. Etienne Gilson, the Catholic historian of medieval philosophy, for example, recognizes that even Erasmus' touted abdication of philosophy is not complete, while Gilson perceptively surmises the inconsistency of Erasmus:

> Nothing better than such a fact discloses what radical diversity of thought can be hidden under the identity of a formula which express them. On the one side, the Reformer Calvin makes use of the name "Christian philosophy," which the Catholic Erasmus had just brought into or restored to fashion. In fact, both agree to make it a theology . . . The position of Calvin, however differs profoundly from that of Erasmus, inasmuch as it is pure and coherent, whereas that of Erasmus is not . . . If you sincerely condemn philosophy as harmful, says Luther to Erasmus, then admit

first that the nature which it interprets is irremediably corrupted. If you sincerely recommend a "Christian philosophy," says Calvin to Erasmus, then admit that reason contributes nothing to it, and that it is exclusively the work of faith. But the Catholic humanist could deny neither the nature which grace healed, nor the natural light to which faith restored sight. But then what business had he to attack philosophy. Since he was anxious to maintain an order of nature endowed with some religious efficacy, Erasmus had no right to reduce natural theology to faith. Evidently of the two Calvin alone had a right to do so.[17]

While Erasmus is willing to dispense with the quibbling of medieval scholastics to include the theological particulars so important to Luther, he nevertheless is unwilling to abandon the medieval fusion of faith and reason in a broader sense, and thus he argues that reason demands that some constraint upon God must be envisioned, so that He "be good." However, in his conception of Christian philosophy as noted by Gilson, Erasmus, as the notorious critic of a medieval philosophical enterprise, can wrongly appear to have abandoned the reason giving rise to philosophy, as he abandons philosophy.

More importantly, however, if Calvin follows Erasmus in the latter's criticism of philosophy, how can Calvin's idea of the reform of religion nevertheless appear substantially like that of Erasmus, when Erasmus continues to accept the natural reason that Calvin presumably rejects?[18] Is it perhaps the case that in their joint opposition to philosophy proper, they nonetheless retain a rational philosophical consciousness that explains their joint opposition to the material element of religious devotion?[19]

To address this question more fully, it is necessary to provide more clarification to Calvin's view of reason and rationality. My contention is

17. Gilson, *Christianity and Philosophy*, 18–19.

18. Eire, *Idols*, 28: "Regarding the issue of worship, or piety, a clear line can be traced between Erasmus and the Reformed tradition. Though Erasmus, the sardonic pacifist, could not stomach the 'virulence' of Protestant iconoclasts, he was at heart in agreement with some of their basic assumptions regarding worship. The search for the roots of the Reformed Protestant attitude toward worship must begin with Erasmus, since it is he who gave rise to a new Christian interpretation of the relationship between the spiritual and the material."

19. On this point note Scavizzi, *Controversy on Images*, 92: "It is ironic that Erasmus and Zwingli—who had staged a war on behalf of a renascence of Christian ideals against what they called paganism—defended the pagans against the current interpretation of their religion; but their defense was not accidental, because their idea of paganism did not indicate a historical era but a way of living and thinking."

that Calvin's position on proper religious devotion is essentially as averse to the material element of religious devotion as the position of Erasmus on material religion. However, is this sideling of the senses for true religion reconcilable with the fact that in Calvin the seat of proper religious devotion appears to lie in the "heart," and not the intellect, the latter too exalted by the medieval scholastics, according to Calvin? In addition, we must give some attention to Calvin's emphasis upon the illumination of the Holy Spirit as the vehicle of faith, for with explicit reference to Scripture, Calvin makes the claim that no argument or proof seals the assurance of its divine origin to the believer, save the inner testimony of the Holy Spirit:

> We ask not for proofs or probabilities on which to rest our judgment, but we subject our intellect and judgment to it as too transcendent for us to estimate. This, however, we do, not in the manner in which some are wont to fasten on an unknown object, which as soon as known, displeases, but because we have a thorough conviction that, in holding it, we hold unassailable truth; not like miserable men, whose minds are inslaved by superstition, but because we feel a divine energy living and breathing in it—an energy by which we are drawn and animated to obey it, willingly indeed, and knowingly, but more vividly and effectually than could be done by human will or knowledge.[20]

This statement might seem far removed from any link to rationalism that I have suggested. To consider the question in its wholeness, however, we must look at how Calvin differentiates his own view from that of the medieval Catholic Schoolmen:

> Hence without the illumination of the Spirit the word has no effect; and hence also it is obvious that faith is something higher than human understanding. Nor were it sufficient for the mind to be illumined by the Spirit of God unless the heart also were strengthened and supported by his power. Here the Schoolmen go completely astray, dwelling entirely in their consideration of faith, on the bare simple assent of the understanding, and altogether overlooking confidence and security of heart. Faith is the special gift of God in both ways,—in purifying the mind so as to give it a relish for divine truth, and afterwards in establishing it therein.[21]

---

20. Calvin, *ICR* 31: 96/Beveridge, *Institutes*, Book I: 72–73.
21. Calvin, *ICR* 32: 54/Beveridge, *Institutes*, Book III: 499.

According to Calvin, therefore, the whole human being must be the recipient of the understanding provided by the Holy Spirit. Calvin contends here that the medieval Schoolmen had a notion of faith concerning something less than the whole person. Calvin's intent, moreover, is to affirm that true religious devotion must penetrate the heart as well as the mind. For Calvin "The Word is not received in faith when it merely flutters in the brain, but when it has taken deep root in the heart, and becomes an invincible bulwark to withstand and repel all the assaults of temptation."[22] In this context, Calvin frequently uses *cor* or "heart" to carry essentially the same meaning as *anima* or "soul." In contrast to his use of *mens* or "mind," the former term refers to "the seat of the emotions," other times described as "the whole range of human affections."

Many Calvin scholars have taken this as indicative, and correctly so, that "Calvin's insistence on the linkage of mind and heart in faith appears to be a statement concerning the necessity of involving the whole person."[23] Consciously standing in the biblical prophetic tradition, Calvin does not want a divide made in the life of the believer, so as to specify what part of the believer carries the believing. To do so would mean that the believer does not present all of himself or his whole life to God. Thus, the ritualist cannot exhaust his religious devotion in ritual practices alone, undertaken as separable from the rest of life. Furthermore, Calvin is cognizant of the depth of the meaning of "heart" in the Old Testament and insists that the religious life must be extended to the whole of the human person and all of life. Therefore, when Calvin uses the word *cor* in reference to religious devotion, his general intent is explicitly not to exclude something else (such as *mens*), but to include everything. Any preference he may appear to exhibit for the *cor* over the *mens* in terms of faith is due to his belief that believers will much more readily "allow themselves to be restricted by numerous severe laws, to be obliged to numerous laborious observances, to wear a severe and heavy yoke; in short, there is no annoyance to which they will not submit, provided there is no mention of the heart."[24] This is the case simply because Calvin is aware of the human propensity to shortchange God in the exercise of various religious practices. In Calvin's mind, the recalcitrant idols of the heart prove to be the most resistant to the practice

---

22. Calvin, *ICR* 32: 57/Beveridge, *Institutes*, Book III: 501.
23. Muller, "*Fides* and *Cognitio*," 219.
24. Calvin, *NRE* 34: 479; Beveridge, *Tracts and Treatises*, Vol. I:154.

of true religion, for humans are greatly moved to resist the practice of real religion and settle on something else requiring less of them than their all.

It is precisely at this point, however, that my contention about the Reformed and like traditions may seem highly disputable. That is, how does the emphasis upon the heart comport with my claim of essentially a rationalist notion of proper religious devotion present in the Reformed tradition? However, I do not claim that in the Reformed tradition there is a shift from heart to head religion due to the neglect of "heart," but rather due to the neglect of materiality. My contention, moreover, arises over the question of whether the Reformed notion of proper religious devotion does in fact ensure the full engagement of the religious devotee as clearly intended in the practice of true religion. That is, just as the ritualist can shortchange God by offering only the outer but not the required inner disposition of true religious devotion, do the attenuated physical components of Reformed religious devotion likewise shortchange the religious devotee of something else essential for human religious devotion to God? A limitation in the Reformed effort at "full" religious devotion I contend occurs; the Reformed notion of true religion carries an eroding rationalism that places the material components of human beings largely outside religious life. This is why the Reformed effort at true religion starts to look uncannily like philosophers engaged in religious devotion.

The Protestant attempt to wean religious devotion and piety away from the material and sensual has been judged almost as uniformly as the shortcomings of the material nature of medieval piety.[25] That is, just as the luxurious material expression of faith in the Catholic Middle Ages lead to aberrant forms of religious faith—idolatry, superstition—so too, the Protestant intent to move religious devotion away from material aids is seen as evidence of rational infiltration in the religious reforms of the Protestant Reformers.[26] My contention, however, is that this rationalism is indicative of a consciousness more properly characterized as philosophical rather than as religious—despite the aversion of many Protestant Reformers toward formal philosophy.

Moreover, the particular Protestant emphasis upon religious experience is not incongruous with the rational inclination of the Reformed tradition, for it is precisely the experiential expectation within Reformed

---

25. Dickens, *The English Reformation*, 11.

26. For example, see Huizinga, *Waning Middle Ages*, 284; Christensen, *Art and the Reformation*, 18.

religion making the restricting rationalism so noticeable. That is, Reformed religious practice begins to resemble philosophers negotiating for a path outside the world. Indeed, this appearance is suggested in the not atypical words of Catholic historian Christopher Dawson, who, like others, has characterized the transition between Medieval Catholicism and Protestantism as one in which "the Reformers raised the standard of religious knowledge and practice by exclusively intellectual and rational means."[27] The point made here by Dawson, however, must be explicated further to understand how the Protestant emphasis on experience is comingled with rationalism.

John E. Smith, an astute observer of Protestant thought, has correctly noted on this point that

> A typical stereotype of Protestantism is that it is passionate, evangelical, and an expression of individual feeling in contrast to the imposing philosophical theologies of the Middle Ages. The truth is that having denied the authority of the Pope and the magisterium, the Reformed Churches stood in need of a new source of unity and authority. The result was the appeal to the Bible, to Creeds and Confessions and to new systems of theology as means of establishing unity and identity among the Reformed Churches. In short, contrary to popular conceptions, Protestantism became quite rationalistic in the centuries after Luther . . .[28]

I of course am claiming that the rationalistic base was laid in the century of Luther, the sixteenth century, and significantly by Reformed thinkers. If this is the case, then rationalism is not only a development of later Protestantism, as Smith's assertion leans, but in part, there from the beginning in sectors of Protestantism. My extended thesis would therefore claim that later forms of Reformed Protestantism became increasingly affectional and in many cases anti-intellectual after the squeezing of the senses and the heavily cognitive nature of early Reformed religion. Thus I assign some significant origins of this rationalism to the Reformed tradition of the sixteenth century. Smith is correct to note, in his next sentence of the prior referenced work, that Protestant rationalism, which he sees as present in the Puritans, provoked a response: "The reaction to this state of affairs, not unlike the reaction of Romanticism to the rationalism of the Enlightenment in Europe, took the form of a new appeal to individual experience, to feeling

---

27. Dawson, *Dividing of Christendom*, 210.
28. Smith, *Jonathan Edwards*, 7.

Protestantism and Rationalism

and to what [Jonathan] Edwards called 'heart' religion" (7). In particular, it is later forms of Protestant religion—highly affectional, sometimes exceedingly experiential, and often anti-intellectual—that invoke most skepticism over the assertion of rationalism in Reformed religion.

Most doubt over aligning Protestants with intellectualism and rationalism is due to focus upon later Protestants in reaction against such intellectualism which calls to mind, however and again, historically later forms of Protestantism. Examples would be German pietism—which was a response to Protestant scholasticism—and American revivalism—a response to American Reformed Puritanism. In these reactions to a perceived rationalism, "heart" is of uppermost importance in religious experience. These "heart" religions, moreover, are sometimes conceived from rebellion against "head" religion. An even later, and thus more recent example, incorporating not only heart religion, but "body" religion, would be the speaking in tongues, healings, and miracles of the twentieth century Pentecostal tradition of Protestantism.[29] However, in the mix of various Protestantisms, Jaroslav Pelikan has written that "The Protestant Reformation was launched by a cadre of intellectuals, but the latter-day heirs of the Reformation sometimes seem determined to do everything they can to live down this past."[30]

Forms of Protestantism are particularly suspicious of "externals" as spiritual or devotional helps, for they present the peril of standing in the place of Christ. This suspicion is accountable to the more or less strong prophetic element of Protestantism and also a perpetual worry of the Reformers—that aids to worship instead of Christ would come to be thought of as necessary for salvation, thus endangering the doctrine of *sola fide*. To guard even more against such a potential peril, in Reformed thought, reference to Christ was often to the "naked Christ."[31] This almost reductive emphasis upon Christ as spiritual, however, can elicit a response of desensualized human spirituality. An attempt may be made to conflate the individual human religious practitioner to the same metaphysical—that is spiritual modality—of God. Materiality, therefore may have little place in this configuration of the relation of finite to infinite spirit. In Reformed thought, the argument against images, for example, is often an objection

---

29. I owe reminder of this point to Rev. Dr. Tom Duncan.

30. Pelikan, *The Christian Intellectual*, 17.

31. Calvin, for example, in *The Necessity of Reforming the Church*, often refers to spiritual truth as "naked and simple."

to the *material* depiction of the infinite God, for the fact that God is spirit is thought to provide a point of congruence between the finite and infinite spirit. What recedes in this desire for similitude, naturally, is the significance of the material component of the finite creature, a component now largely sidelined because there is no perceived corresponding element in the creator, with Christ therefore being understood transcendentally, and rarely incarnationally.

Calvin's criticism of the Schoolmen is lodged against an *excessively* intellectual view of proper religious faith. However, Calvin's criticism is also a criticism found in the Schoolmen, for the Scholastics had typically guarded the faith from the "bare simple assent of the understanding" by distinguishing between knowledge, assent, and trust. Not even Aquinas presents the view that faith is merely a matter of assent to knowledge, but rather expresses the view that the intellect and the will are conjoined in faith. Whether Calvin is unaware of this view among the Scholastics I am not aware, but his general distaste for medieval thinkers in general is well known. Moreover, perhaps what may have provoked Calvin into the charge against the Schoolmen was the notion of *fides implicita*. Against this notion Calvin's criticism might find its mark.

> Hence, in order that the word of God may gain full credit, the mind must be enlightened, and the heart confirmed, from some other quarter. We shall now have a full definition of faith if we say that it is a firm and sure knowledge of the divine favour toward us, founded on the truth of a free promise in Christ, and revealed to our minds, and sealed on our hearts, by the Holy Spirit . . . And first, I must refute the nugatory distinction of the Schoolmen as to formed and unformed faith . . . But we must first see whether any one can by his own strength acquire faith, or whether the Holy Spirit, by means of it, becomes the witness of adoption. Hence it is childish trifling in them to inquire whether the faith formed by the supervening quality of love be the same, or a different and new faith . . . Did they duly ponder the saying of Paul, 'With the heart man believeth unto righteousness' (Rom. x. 10), they would cease to dream of that frigid quality. There is one consideration which ought at once to put an end to the debate—viz. that assent itself is more a matter of the heart than the head, of the affection than the intellect.[32]

---

32. Calvin, *ICR* 32: 18–19/Beveridge, *Institutes*, Book III: 475–76.

Here Calvin's criticism of "mere assent" might find resonance in the notion of implicit faith. In this passage, Calvin seems to locate the center of religious activity in the heart and in the affections, contrasted to their counterparts. In this sense, then, Calvin is using *heart* here as a component of the human person to be contrasted to its counterpart the head, and thus is used to indicate the whole person. However, this move does not jeopardize my thesis because when Calvin uses the word *heart* as a term of contrast with the head or intellect, this places Calvin's notion of religious devotion no closer to the things of sensibility and materiality—despite the traditional association of affections, for example, with the material body.

To evidence this point more, another comparison is helpful. In comparing the Reformed thinkers to Luther, one finds in Luther's famous slur upon reason as the whore, and in his desire to expunge philosophy from theology,[33] no comparable fulminations against the use of the material element in religious devotion. With a view different from the Reformed thinkers on the appropriateness of materiality in religious practice, Luther also exhibits more severity—and more consistency—toward philosophy. Of all the major Protestant Reformers, Luther has the highest view of the "externals"—art, ritual, and liturgy—coupled with the lowest view of philosophy. This includes his view of images as *adiaphora* or things indifferent, as well as holding the highest view of any of the Reformers on the "real presence" of Christ in the Eucharist. Luther's views stand in stark contrast to Zwingl's famous statement that in the realm of religious devotion, "What you give the senses you take away from the Spirit."[34] This contrast between the Reformed thinkers and Luther prompts the obvious question whether it is more than coincidence that Luther—who of the major Reformers was most hostile to philosophy—was also the one most receptive to the use of the material element in religious devotion. Specifically, what is it in philosophy that Luther rejects, but that seems to be embraced in Karlstadt, Zwingli, and Calvin as early Reformed thinkers?

In refusing to polarize the body and the spirit, Luther's reform takes a turn fundamentally different from that seen in Erasmus and Calvin, where

---

33. Luther makes probably his most disparaging comments against philosophy in his *Disputation Against Scholastic Theology*, published in 1517. As noted by Ozment, however, though Luther criticized heavily the use of Aristotle in theology, he could see that Erasmus, who also criticized the incorporation of philosophy in theology, nevertheless retained underlying sympathy with much medieval theology that was based on philosophical notions that Luther— but not Erasmus, opposed.

34. Letter from Zwingli to Bucer, dated 3 June, 1524, in *CR* 95: 195. The original text reads "*Iam hoc non ignoras, quod, quantum sensui tribueris, tantum spiritui detraxeris.*"

disparagement of the material components of religious devotion polarizes the religious devotee.[35] Luther looks with disfavor upon any juxtaposing of the external from the internal calculated to sever the two. The Reformed tradition, with antecedents in thinkers like Erasmus and Karlstadt, seems to take another view. I maintain that a substantial key to the difference between these two Protestant traditions on the use of the material element in religious devotion is traceable to the implicit rationalism evident in the early Reformed thinkers, but cautiously avoided by Luther. This becomes apparent as the Reformed thinkers find their aversion to any image or picture of deity corroborated by pagan philosophers, but also in the way that their view of "true religion" resonates in the implicit rationalism of the philosophical consciousness.

Notably, the charge of "rationalism" is one that Luther leveled against his initial friend and colleague but later virulent opponent, Andreas Karlstadt, whose spiritualism Luther deplored, though it would eventually find acceptance in the Reformed thinkers. In Luther's pamphlet written specifically against acts of iconoclastic destruction influenced by Karlstadt's spiritualism, it is significant that he repeatedly repudiates Karlstadt's brand of religiosity, which Luther deems calculated to provide an erroneous antithesis between body and spirit:

> Thus, whoever follows Dr. Karlstadt's opinions must fall between two chairs and be suspended between heaven and earth . . . I have often asserted that the ultimate goal of the devil is to do away with the entire sacrament and all outward ordinances of God. Then as these prophets [Karlstadt and others] teach, all that would count would be for the hearer to stare inwardly at the spirit. Everyone now clearly sees, I think, that Dr. Karlstadt's spirit is one that seeks to fool the people with the word "spiritual," and undertakes to make everything spiritual which God has made bodily . . . The pope has lied in the same manner. But his spirit has rather busied itself in making spiritual things bodily, as he transforms a spiritual Christendom into an outward bodily community. This sectarian spirit, on the other hand, is mostly concerned about making spiritual what God has made bodily and outward. We therefore proceed between the two, making nothing spiritual or bodily, but

---

35. The infamous cultural historian Norman O. Brown even goes so far as to claim of Luther that "psychoanalysis must recognize that [Luther's] repudiation of all efforts to rise above the body is if anything more consistent than Freud's." Brown, *Life Against Death*, 232.

in keeping spiritual what God makes spiritual, and bodily what he makes bodily.[36]

More instances of Luther's disdain for rational "spiritualizers" could be cited, but this passage samples how Luther, and much of later Lutheranism,[37] stand to a great degree outside the tendency to rationalism often prominent in Protestant religion. In fact, the notable theories of Max Weber,[38] concerning the rise of capitalism, and Robert Merton,[39] concerning the rise of science, predicated on the basis of a detectable rationalism in Protestantism and Puritanism, explicitly separated their contentions from the Lutheran tradition. In many ways, Lutheran receptivity to the material has been significant enough to enable one to see a greater relationship in its practices of religious devotion, to Catholicism, rather than to the Reformed or Anabaptist and Free Church traditions of Protestantism.

While it is true that Luther, like the other early Protestant Reformers, elevates the word and hearing of the word to the highest position as a vehicle of religious understanding, he refuses to sever the other senses as vehicles for understanding the word.[40] Luther's embrace of the material element in religious devotion provokes notice of his disdain for spiritualizing rationalism in religion. By contrast, one sees in Reformed Protestant-

---

36. Luther, *Against the Heavenly Prophets*, 191–92.

37. Rudolf Otto, in his *Idea of the Holy*, 108, has high marks for Luther, but disparages much later Lutheranism "whose only life is in the conscious mental attitude of the devout soul." Hegel, as one of these later Lutherans, is heavily criticized by Otto, 92.

38. Max Weber, *The Protestant Ethic*, 86: "He [Luther] could not but suspect the tendency to ascetic self-discipline of leading to salvation by works, and hence he and his Church were forced to keep it more and more in the background. Thus the mere idea of the calling in the Lutheran sense is at best of questionable importance for the problem in which we are interested." Weber also notes, 127, that in Lutheranism one "finds few parallels in genuine Puritanism."

39. Robert K. Merton, *Science, Technology and Society*, 58: "Perhaps the one major Protestant variation from the Puritan ethos is afforded by Lutheranism, with its precepts of justification by faith only and its emphasis on penitent grief, but since this sect had no appreciable influence on English life, this divergence is of no importance."

40. It is clearly the case that, for Luther, words are of more importance both theologically and psychologically for religious devotion. However, a reading of Luther against Karlstadt reveals that he regards the severance of the other senses from religious experience as completely at variance with human ways of knowing. Furthermore, the famous "subjectivity" in Luther's thought ("Christ for me") pushes him away from questions about the essence of God and toward the appropriation of the role of Christ in the life of the believer. Similarly, he devotes no time to the essence of religious art, but instead asks what it can do for the believer seeking to draw close to Christ.

ism, beginning in Zwingli, but also evident in Calvin, the combination of a greater receptivity to philosophy (though ancient and not medieval philosophy), coinciding with a revulsion against the use of sensual elements in religious devotion. The precise opposite has been noted in Luther. This great difference between these two Protestant traditions on this question is why one may evaluate the Reformed hesitancy toward materiality as the catalyst of a "Second Reformation."

The Philosophical Consciousness in Reformed Religion

Calvin, in his chapter on images in the *Institutes*, is almost apologetic that he has the backing of certain ancient philosophers who shunned the idea of sensuality in the depiction of deity.[41] Zwingli's successor Bullinger, in his *De Origine Erroris*,[42] a work Calvin was to rely upon in successive editions of the *Institutes*, found an historical link with these philosophers, though pagans, in their revulsion toward sensual depictions in religious practices. This link with the pagan philosophers gave Bullinger license to see the Old Testament Commandment against images and sensual representation as embedded in consciousness strongly enough to refer to it as a natural law. The Reformed Protestants now saw their theology in part corroborated from the pagan philosophers, but not with the ancient pagan commoners, whom they saw as analogous to the medieval populace—steeped in the idolatry of sensuality and materiality. This distinction has obvious import: that such material aids are for the weak of faith. The link severed and the link established with ancient paganism reveal that Reformed thinkers found favor with a significant party in the ancient world: the rational philosophers.

The use of images in religious devotion became particularly prominent in medieval Catholicism after Gregory the Great and was propelled in part because of the credence given to image use in Gregory's famous statement that "images are the books of the unlearned." I know of no major Protestant Reformer, who after weighing this assertion, did not rebuke

---

41. "And surely it is disgraceful that heathen writers should be more skillful interpreters of Scripture than the Papists. Juvenal (*Sat.* xiv.) holds up the Jews to derision for worshipping the thin clouds and firmament. This he does perversely and impiously; still, in denying that any visible shape of deity existed among them, he speaks more accurately than the Papists, who prate about there having been some visible image." *ICR* 31: 123/ Beveridge, *Institutes*, Book I: 93.

42. Heinrich Bullinger, *De Origine Erroris*, 1529.

Gregory for it.[43] Calvin, for example, despised Gregory's dictum because Calvin made no gradations among the faithful that would allow for any tailoring of devotion based upon individual religious understanding or need. Calvin's solution to the "unlearned" is that they be properly taught, thus throwing out the cloak of ignorance that image devotion encourages among the faithful.

Nevertheless, Calvin does not think that all Christian believers are susceptible to the idolatry that the use of images encourages, but he does link susceptibility toward the error of using images with how one thinks about God. In Calvin's mind, the demarcation between the truth and error on this important point is not a simple contrast between pagan and Christian, but rather between right and wrong notions of deity that exclude or permit the use of material images in religious devotion. Thus, the argument about images is pushed to a transcendental plane that levels both pagan and Christian error on this point. There is, consequently, no reason that Christian thinkers cannot use astute pagan thinkers in the effort to eradicate the error.

It is hardly a surprise to find that Calvin, in approaching the issue of images and material media in devotional practice, paid little attention to the traditional Christological discussion that often accompanied the issue of images. That is, while most advocates for the use of images in the Christian history of the question had framed the discussion around God having taken on human flesh in the Incarnation, Calvin, however, speaks almost exclusively about images as being an insult and abomination to God. This at least suggests that Calvin's position on images might hold without distinction between the conceptual god of the philosophers—certainly immaterial—and the incarnate historical God in Christ. Zwingli admitted that the traditional argument referencing the Incarnation was the "greatest obstacle" to the opposer of images.[44] Karlstadt, likewise, governs his opposition to images from a theocentric rather than a Christocentric perspective.

43. Luther is the exception. Michalski, *Reformation*, 29, points out that "He even wrote about children and simple folk that 'they are moved more by an image and an allegory than by mere words or doctrines, as St. Mark attests.' Especially significant was his remark about 'images for children and simple folk.' This indirect reference to the famous pronouncement of Gregory the Great about images as 'books for the unlearned' was a clearly Catholicizing point of view in the dispute of the 1520s." Walker, *History*, 157, writes, "To some extent it made the way from heathenism to Christianity easier for thousands, but it even stood in danger of heathenizing the church itself."

44. To my knowledge, Zwingli never addressed the argument of John of Dasmascus for icons, however.

Calvin's argument against images, in which he links the argument of the pagan with his own argument for the unchanging eternal essence of God, is clearly exhibited in a passage from the *Institutes:*

> Seneca's complaint, as given by Augustine, *De Civit. Dei,* c. 10, is well known. He says, "The sacred, immortal, and invisible gods, they exhibit in the meanest and most ignoble materials, and dress them in the clothing of men and beasts; some confound the sexes, and form a compound out of different bodies, giving the name of deities to objects, which, if they were met alone, would be deemed monsters." Hence, again, it is obvious, that the defenders of images resort to a paltry quibbling evasion, when they pretend that the Jews were forbidden to use them on account of their proneness to superstition; as if a prohibition which the Lord founds on his own eternal essence, and the uniform course of nature, could be restricted to a single nation.[45]

This passage makes more understandable Calvin's appeal to ancient philosophers who similarly felt an affront in giving God visible or sensual form. This appeal, however, is weak because a philosopher who could not admit an incarnate God can scarcely underwrite the view that an incarnate God should not be depicted visually.

To some degree Calvin's reticence toward images and other material aids resonates from a theology that attempts to transform a religion of immanence into a religion of transcendence. "Spiritual" understanding produces the same effect. Calvin's heavy critique of miracles attributed to images is followed by a severe critique of miracles on principle. The attempt to give God a sensual representation compromises the majesty of God while the miracles often associated with images mingle the supernatural and sensuality in a way abhorrent to Calvin. Particularly because of the latter, Calvin, in a sense, curbs the supernatural and the miraculous away from the ordinary world while moving the purpose of miracles to the realm of adjudicating revelation. Carlos Eire has observed with acumen that, with little alteration, what Galileo said of Copernicus could be applied to Calvin and his followers: "'They were able,' he said 'to make reason so conquer sense that, in defiance of the latter, the former became the mistress of their belief.'"[46]

---

45. *ICR* 31: 120–21/Beveridge, *Institutes,* Book I: 92.
46. Eire, *Idols,* 311–12.

Protestantism and Rationalism

Calvin of course does not deny, but rather affirms, the role of the affections in rightly knowing God. However, typical of the broader shift of Reformation religious sensibility, he differs from medieval Catholicism in regarding which senses correctly arouse and sustain that knowledge of God. Calvin's opposition to images is in great part due to his juxtaposition of the image to the word and of the eye to the ear. The concentration upon the word and upon hearing then lead in a natural manner to a religious practice which can easily become chiefly cerebral. Coupled with this concentration is Calvin's strong emphasis upon a transcendent God which lends itself easily to an intellectualist mode of religious devotion. God is a Spirit is a Mind.[47] Thus, this religious sensibility will train the mind, while being wary of the use of the emotions.

Though the Reformed view of God, as it works its way from Calvin to Barth, insists upon the transcendence of God as "Wholly Other," humans are nonetheless and paradoxically very much like God in Reformed thought in another way. Zwingli, for example, in a particularly revealing remark, writes, "The common people think that God is placated by victims of cattle and by corporeal things. But even since God himself is spirit: mind: not body, it is obvious that like rejoices in like: doubtless he is above all to be worshipped by purity of mind. And today the mass of Christians worship God through certain corporeal ceremonies; whereas the piety of mind is the most pleasing worship. For the father seeks such worshippers as will worship him in spirit, since he is spirit."[48]

---

47. William J. Bouwsma in his biography of Calvin goes so far as to contend that Calvin on occasion made the implicit move from "the identification of the biblical God with the God of the philosophers." But especially notable among the other insights of Bouwsma's book pertinent to our subject is his contention that "Nominalism has sometimes been represented as a biblically oriented reaction against Hellenic and Arab determinism. But although the God of nominalism may be closer to the Bible in some respects than the God of High Scholasticism, he is also the end product of the long reaction, begun by the Greeks, of philosophy against mythology." Bouwsma, *John Calvin*, 105–6. Interestingly here nominalism is positioned as heir to Greek philosophy as against mythology and for transcendence. Umberto Eco, in *Art and Beauty, 53*, in commenting upon the resurgence of images, relics, and shrines in the medieval period writes, "It was a prolongation of the mythopoeic dimension of the Classical period, though elaborated in terms of the new images and values of the Christian ethos. And again, it was a revival, caused by a new sense of the supernatural, of the sense of wonder which had faltered in late Antiquity when the gods of Lucian replaced the gods of Homer." As regards the Greek satirist Lucian, Erasmus made a translation of Lucian, whose spirit carries over into Erasmus' own *Colloquies* and his satirical *Praise of Folly*.

48. Quoted in Garside, *Zwingli and the Arts*, 37. This is a penned comment of

Denuded Devotion to Christ

The contentions of Zwingli have much significance; persons are separated from God by an intervening material component, and lesser intellects do not realize the import of this fact. Modal reciprocity between spirits is a key in the relation between God and humans. However, sin had been the chasm of separation in the unlikeness between God and humans as conceived with contrasting Reformers such as Luther. In another figure of this shift, there is a submerging or exchange of redemption in Christ for the rational union with the transcendental God. For the relation between God and humans to work, there must be an identity somewhere in divine-human relation. The identity in Zwingli's conception, however, is scarcely or barely between the incarnate Christ and embodied persons, but positioned between a transcendental God and persons aspiring to transcend the world of matter in Christian religious devotion. Whereas Luther had insisted that he knew only the Christ of the flesh, Zwingli in a manner reverses this.

Zwingli's, found in the margins of his copy of Erasmus's *Lucubrationes*. The original text of Zwingli's comment, supplied by Garside reads "*Vulgas existimat deum placari victimis pecudum rebusque corporeis. Verum etiam cumque deus ipse sit animus: mens: non corpus, consentaneum est simile gaudere simili: nimirum potissimum colendus est puritate mentis. Et hodie vulgus Christianorum corporeis quibusdam caerimoniis colit deum: cum gratissimus cultus sit animi pietas. Tales enim adoratores quaerit pater, qui in spiritu adorent, cum ipse sit spiritus.*"

4

The Aesthetic in the Practice of True Religion

The Problem of Religious Understanding

ONE PREDOMINANT TRAIT GOVERNS THE ROLE OF THE AESTHETIC IN Reformed religious devotion: simplicity is to be preferred. The clarity of simplicity functions to attenuate a lusher aesthetic because the goal of simplicity serves the larger Reformed perspective of aiding and not hindering religious understanding.[1] Clarity will be expressed in aesthetic simplicity and not confusing clutter.

This aesthetic exhibits an inclination toward what I have termed "naked truth," in order to aid religious understanding. Fuller development of this notion comes later with the Reformed tradition of the next century, as the English Puritan tradition peeled away more unnecessary layers faulted as masking and hiding the truth beneath mountains of ceremonies, rituals, and other diversions. As an example of this desired aesthetic, William Haller, a prominent historian of the Puritans, cites a Puritan preacher who warned, "Truth feareth nothing so much as concealment, and desireth nothing so much as clearly to be laid open to the view of all: When it is most naked it is most lovely and powerful."[2] This kind of aesthetic resonates and is implied in the bareness of Zwingli's whitewashed church walls,

---

1. The Catholic tradition has less trouble with materiality than Protestantism, though granted because it has a higher tolerance for error. In the Reformed tradition, fear of error often matches desire for truth, and thus it is to be expected that fear of error in some sense turns into a fear for truth. The Catholic tradition in its desire to see the fullness of truth articulated is not stopped by the fact that full articulation often borders on and lapses into idolatry or error.

2. Haller, *The Rise of Puritanism*, 140.

and is affirmed as enhancing religious understanding without ambiguity or subtlety.

However, if it is the case that "the special gift of art is not doctrinal precision, conceptual clarity, or the ability to think straight,"[3] then art eschewing subtlety may explain the insistence upon simplicity in the Reformed aesthetic. Thus, the desire for simplicity is in great part favored so as to resist the temptation toward subtlety. Granted, the subtle component in art may prove more confusing than enlightening to some. What Iris Murdoch writes of Plato's reticence toward art perhaps finds resonance in the Reformed thinkers: "Indirectness and irony prevent the immediate relationship with truth which occurs in live discourse; art is thus the enemy of dialectic."[4]

From the perspective of simplicity, moreover, in poetry or in ritual, there may be judged a husk or blinder that needs to be pulled off so as to expose plainly and clearly the truth for understanding. Poetry and rituals, through the glorification of metaphors and the role of ambiguity, hide and deflect truth's power by overlayering the image more than conveying the message. Therefore, the husk of ritual or the image, either visual or poetic, may be pushed aside. Such things may have come to show the way, but now they are in the way, as Hegel might say, as he contends about history

3. Brown, *Religious Aesthetics*, 167.
4. Murdoch, *Fire and the Sun*, 65. The fear for truth is profitable compared to Nietzsche's criticism of Socrates and Euripides. In Nietzsche's perspective, the subtlety employed by the Greek tragedians was suspect to Euripides because the observer was apt to miss the essential movements of the drama, and thus Euripides employed a most unartful device to remove all ambiguity: "The Euripidean prologue may serve to illustrate the efficacy of that rationalistic method. Nothing could be more at odds with our dramaturgic notions than the prologue in the drama of Euripides. To have a character appear at the beginning of the play, tell us who he is, what preceded the action, what has happened so far, even what is about to happen in the course of the play—a modern writer for the theatre would reject all this as a wanton and unpardonable dismissal of the element of suspense," Nietzsche, *Birth of Tragedy*, 79. The point here is that art is feared for a subtlety that can mask or hide truth. Euripides, as the rational Socratic dramatist, was suspicious of the tragedians who left "something incommensurable in every feature and in every line of the tragedy, a certain deceptive distinctness and at the same time a mysterious depth, almost an infinitude of background. Even the clearest figure always had a comet's tail attached to it, which seemed to suggest the uncertain, the nebulous," 83. In the eyes of Nietzsche Euripides held that "To be beautiful everything must be intelligible." This Nietzsche refers to as the "aesthetic Socrates." Nietzsche's view of the death of Greek tragedy serves to make the point that the subtlety of art may defy understanding and that the insistence on understanding may purge art to the point that scarcely any art, and perhaps less mystery, remains.

The Aesthetic in the Practice of True Religion

and religious objects. The critic may nevertheless admit that there is truth embodied—though submerged or buried—in the ritual of the ritualist, but to him the "embodiment" is a distraction rather than a service. Such things perform a disservice to the deeper and also clearer truth—surely capable of being shown simply as truth or as "naked truth." To the critic, an unnecessary duplicity is present in the example of ritual: this is why the truth in the ritual must be shorn of the ritual to find or see the point. What may be deemed most alluring, but manifestly failing at directing the worshipper to the right end, according to the ritual critic, is the ritual itself. This argument, in some form, is the charge against subtlety. In other words, the argument may be simply an insistence upon the necessity of bareness—or nakedness again—in order to see clearly.

The keen desire to avoid error and to lay truth bare has not made Reformed Protestantism venturesome in regard to the use of the arts in religion, but to view them through the lens of the same suspicions with which most material components of religious devotion are viewed. Art, as in Plato, is suspect because it is not nor can it be as discerning or discriminating in the necessary conflict and distinctions drawn between truth and error as can dialectic and discursive reasoning. The theological task, then, will be undertaken largely as an exercise with the verbal sensibilities. Other sensibilities are judged to lack the clarity and capacity of verbal discourse and distinctions; such a culture will likely produce more philosophers or scientists than poets or painters.

With primary devotion trusting most in the verbal sensibility, what is often missing is the power of subtlety—though suspicious to Calvin—that is captured by art and that provides some of the power of the aesthetic. Thus, art may shoulder or present a message more powerfully than directions or dictated words in some contexts. Indeed, even the critics of art would generally concede this point.[5] But words may be perceived as, on one account, the clearest means of reference to the absent. Moreover, they may also be presumed to be the safest, for words can be retracted, rebuked, and policed faster than aesthetic perceptions that may permeate at times the deepest levels of consciousness. Furthermore, as remarked by John W. Dixon, there is an unrecognized weakness about the versatility of words: "There is a particular cogency to the verbal and conceptual system which

---

5. This characterization of art is that art is, on all points of view, powerful. The perceived weakness is a function of the power: art can attach its power to truth or error. For this reason, Murdoch, in *The Fire and the Sun*, 69–70, makes the point that, "Art may here be seen as the more 'dangerous' where 'pure thought' is less powerful."

gives it the appearance of primacy. It can be argued, manipulated, as the others cannot, and this increases its popularity. But the system can cover only part of experience."[6]

However, if we are to work to avoid subtlety in order to avoid error, what may be substituted is a keen concentration on words because they are perceived as the clearest route to the avoidance of error and also the greatest clarifier and protector of truth. For this reason, theological creeds might be seen and faulted for casting the impression of an exclusion of understanding compared to other modes of understanding or apprehension, because the creeds have most often been viewed as the apex of theological understanding and reflection. It must be noted, however, that the point at issue is not the verbal or non-verbal nature of the theological task, but whether the verbal sensibility can accommodate other sensibilities left largely sidelined by verbal predominance.

The Reformed thinkers' view of art concedes the power of art, but the power of art comes across in their estimation as a negative power. That is, inasmuch as the desire for objects that resonate with the senses explains the lure of art, from the Reformed perspective, the appetite for such things issues from the weaker part of the human. More specifically, the desire for material forms for religious devotion reflects the sensual craving for sensual objects and is hardly an aid to a religious practice trying to lift itself from things material. It is for this reason that Auksi can hardly characterize more succinctly or accurately the difference between Luther and Calvin on religious devotion than a difference in which "Luther is willing and eager to adapt matter to spirit, while Calvin seeks to lessen the human need for sensuous stimulation in order to intensify spirit."[7] We also encounter Calvin's admission that ritual has to do primarily with the body, as he stringently curbs ceremony and ritual—because of the affiliation with the physical. As noted before, and particularly with Zwingli, religious faith and devotion should be utterly unrelated to anything involving the senses. Given such examples of this dichotomy between matter and spirit, Margaret Aston, in speaking of the early Reformed perspective on true religion, seems not far off the mark with her contention that "Physical erasure was part of the vitalizing ferment of the new age."[8]

---

6. Dixon, *Nature and Grace*, 14–15.
7. Auksi, "Simplicity and Silence," 216.
8. Ashton, *England's Iconoclasts*, 10.

The Aesthetic in the Practice of True Religion

The Material in Art

Religious reform appears to imperil the place for the aesthetic, for it is notable that suspicions about the aesthetic have had some of their most intense expressions within movements of religious reform. Within Christianity, some reformers seeking to strenuously augment religious devotion have delimited or disengaged material possible for aesthetic use. The general Protestant objection might seem to assume that as the individual spiritually matures, he requires less need for material things to augment spiritual understanding. He may be judged to advance in religious maturity by fewer things being required—particularly fewer embodied or material aids—than his historical predecessors apparently required. For Calvin, moreover, the joining of art to religion, whether in the form of images, *cultus decorum*, or lavish ceremony, is indication of the feebleness of false religion— that it need resort to such things. False religion is to be understood as impoverishing religion, because for Calvin, it is a mark of true religion to have little need for things of a physical or material nature.

For pointed historical examples of religion and art poised in opposition, one may view the iconoclastic controversy, or the episode of Savonarola and Florence, or the English Puritans in conflict with the established English church. From a positive perspective of what one might call natural religion, however, the aesthetic would seem to find place as an eventual historical component of religion, such that religion and religious practice would seem to accumulate and encompass aesthetic elements naturally. If this is the case, then, it is when religious practice is under scrutiny and perhaps faulted for perceived excesses that the reform of religion may seek to trim an aesthetic component deemed at some cross purposes with the core of the religion. Nevertheless, the human appetite for the aesthetic, art, and symbolism may be too strong and thus significantly resist this kind of refining and reforming effort. This conjecture seems obvious in the fact that the iconoclasts and Savonarola in their opposition to art suffered stiff resistance, and the Puritans in opposing the art and ritual of the Anglicans were forced from Anglicanism and largely became Separatists.

That art and religion seem to historically manifest some congruity comes as scarcely a surprise to us: we find it difficult to imagine a cave dweller who would venture to have all cave drawings removed in the interest of advancing piety.[9] Any such initial congruity for the early Reformed

---

9. For the early religionist, no conflict between art and religion can arise until

thinkers is apt to be evaluated by them, however, as a general indication of the strong propensity of humans toward idolatry and weak religion. Spiritual religion seems capable of lifting the individual devotee above reliance upon the material components of religion. Such an evaluation also numbers like-minded but pre-Christian thinkers with the same notion, allies on this point, for these thinkers chastized the tendency of their own culture and populations to present visual depictions of deity. From this opposite perspective, the nearly universal human propensity to co-join or fuse materiality to religious practice is faulted as indication of a universal human spiritual frailty, however much it might be defended as natural by others. Therefore, the presence of visible art in religious practice as manifested in earlier stages of both civilization and religion will eventually be judged as indication of not only idolatry, but also the feebleness of early religion. This is a point Hegel emphasizes in his contention that cultural ideas expressed in and through art forms will weaken for humans as conceptualization takes over the expression of the spiritual world.

Therefore and generally speaking, religious conceptions that question and weaken the place for art in religion seem later in the history of religion and begin to arise as a culture approximates a mode of philosophical consciousness, where material form is trumped or sidestepped for conceptualization as a higher and presumably ultimately more satisfying way of understanding or configuring the world. When this transition occurs, religious practice may be altered, to the point of severe truncation, but this change may be positively evaluated as the realization of "true religion." In this historical progression, the place for art will be revisited and perhaps

---

conceptions differentiating the two are present. But as noted by Weber, *Sociology of Religion*, 242–43: "That religion has been an inexhaustible spring of artistic expressions is evident from the existence of idols and icons of every variety . . . But the more art becomes an autonomous sphere, which happens as a result of lay education, the more art tends to acquire its own set of constitutive values, which are quite different from those obtaining in the religious and ethical domain."

In comparison to Protestantism, Catholicism and Eastern Orthodoxy are steeped more deeply in the use of art in religious practice, but not because religion and art continue to remain undifferentiated. Rather, theirs is a conscious decision to use art after art in some degree becomes distinct from religion. Thus, Catholicism admits art and visual art in particular in religious practice in large part because of the Incarnation of Christ, whereas Luther's argument contends that God created us as material as well as spiritual beings. Unlike the case of the cave dweller, however, the handmaiden theory of the arts reflects the nature of a conscious and deliberate alliance, whereas the religious practice of an earlier devotee given to "art" lacks the distinction capable of consciously joining or severing one from the other.

diminished within the province of religion and religious practice. Such a perspective, therefore, eventually contributes to the secularization of art by viewing art as potentially too libelous or simply too primitive for the practice of true or higher religion. This kind of religious worship and practice will necessarily push art toward secular quarters.

The diminution of art can occur on multiple fronts and therefore not simply with regard to its future as a continuing feature of religious life and religious practice, but also as a suitable vehicle for human or religious knowledge. John Dixon, however, has made the point that many have surely raised about the cultural transition from materialization to conceptualization. That is, any claim that judges the non-verbal as primordial and in time regulates it to a lesser function—especially when the human continues with a cultural appetite for it—may prove premature: "The only problem is that other human activities that are non-verbal are considered not to give access to reality . . . The result is that a presentation of works of art to a general audience is more of an entertainment than it is a serious contribution to learning."[10] Hegel's ranking of art beneath religion and philosophy reflects the scrutiny of a philosopher bracketing the value of art in relation to religion and philosophy. Not unlike religion itself, in belonging to the earlier history of humankind, art finds itself often on the defensive in any argument about its future.

In terms of the Reformed perspective, tied as art largely is to physical and material media, for example, Weber's "idols and icons," resistance toward the physical and material easily translates into a similar resistance toward art. Of course, the hesitation and at times outright hostility of the Reformed tradition toward art in religious devotion has been legendary, from the iconoclastic riots and destruction perhaps inspired by the vehemence of Karlstadt to the "beautiful whitewashed walls" of Zwingli's Zurich Church. Ernst Troeltsch, in his *Protestantism and Progress*, therefore concluded that Protestant religious practice, but particularly Reformed Protestant practice, would be a religion largely exercised without exercising art:

> The latter [Protestantism] killed legend and miracle outside the New Testament, and fostered a spirit of unimaginative practicality. That is especially true of Calvinism, for neither the Dutch wholly un-Puritan painting, nor the poetic elements in Milton's Renaissance poetry, are to be put down to its account—still less so Rembrandt, who had more affinity with mystical, spiritualistic circles. Shakespeare, too, in spite of the undoubtedly strong religious

---

10. Dixon, "When Is Art Religion?" 132.

strain in his writing, ought not to be claimed exclusively for Protestant art, as his hatred of the Puritans sufficiently testifies.[11]

But as noted by Max Weber, driving the strong separation of the aesthetic from the religious was a divide between matter and spirit reflected in a transcendental god and an ascetic human: "The more the god proclaimed by the prophets was conceived as transcendental and sacred, the more insoluble and irreconcilable became this opposition between religion and art . . . In all this, the one important fact for us is the significance of the marked rejection of all distinctively esthetic devices by those religions which are rational, in our special sense. These are Judaism, ancient Christianity, and—later on—ascetic Protestantism."[12]

Expanding upon the point made by Weber, Troeltsch contends, "The Augustianism of the Western system of thought, to which the older Protestantism essentially belongs, here yields to a new spiritual power which forever divides the modern world from early Protestantism."[13] The "new spiritual power" referenced by Troeltsch is indication of the desensualizing philosophical consciousness underlying the penchant for the austerities of true religion by the early Reformed thinkers. The "divide" indicated does not discount the role of the Reformed perspective in seeding modernity,

---

11. Troeltsch, *Protestantism and Progress*, 85. In his chapter on John Milton in *The Rise of Puritanism*, Haller, 289, writes of Milton that "Most have agreed, however, that he was, the more the pity, a man somehow at war with himself, the poet and the Puritan within him struggling for mastery and ruling him by turns. Little remains to be said concerning this view of Milton. It may be true but we do not know. What we can truthfully say is that, though he tells us much about himself in relation to his art, he never acknowledges the war between poetry and Puritanism . . ."

12. Weber, *Sociology of Religion*, 242–43.

13. Troeltsch, *Protestantism and Progress*, 85. Troletsch's reference to the modern abandonment of early Protestantism because of the aesthetic issue prompts us to consider another question. If it is the case that there is some agreement between Hegel's philosophical consciousness and the Reformed thinkers conception of true religion as it concerns the material nature of art, then why is it also the case that the eclipse of religion in modernity is not paralleled by an eclipse of art? Indeed, on Hegel's analysis, this would be expected, as he himself famously wrote that "Art remains for us a thing of the past." However, Hegel has not been vindicated on this contention. As noted by Taylor, in his *Hegel*, 479: "For far from taking a second place in the spiritual life of modern man, art has taken over from religion in the lives of many of our contemporaries, in the sense that it is for them the highest expression of what is of ultimate importance, and/or the highest activity of man. And this by itself is an indication of how far we have moved out of the purview of Hegel's synthesis." On the basis of Taylor's analysis, one could conjecture, correctly I believe, that the human appetite for art will resist to varying degrees the contrary desire to subjugate it into conceptualization.

nor in the desacrilization of the world. Rather, the strong Reformed resistance to the material for spiritual purpose positions that tradition at odds with the modern world, however much that tradition contributed secular impetus to the modern scientific conception of the world. Evelyn Underhill's description of the resulting culture of religious worship in the Reformed perspective connotes the exacting resistance of the conceptual philosophical consciousness driving away material and aesthetic components in human religious worship of God.

> In the type of worship which he [Calvin] established, we seem to see the result of a great religious experience—the impact of the Divine Transcendence on the awe-struck soul—and the effort towards a response which is conditioned by a deep sense of creaturely limitation, but deficient in homely and child-like dispositions; and, with intrepid French logic, refuses the use of creaturely aids. Calvin desired, as so many great religious souls have done, a completely spiritual cultus; ascending towards a completely spiritual Reality, and rejecting all the humble ritual methods and all the sensible signs by which men are led to express their adoration of the Unseen. God who "hath no image" was the ultimate fact. Therefore a pitiless lucidity of mind, which ignored the mysterious relation between poetry and reality, and the need of stepping-stones from the successive to the Eternal, insisted that all which is less than God must be abjured when man turns to adoration.[14]

The Sufficiency of Truth

One liability of art is that the strength of the medium, that is, the solicitation of the emotions, for example, can jeopardize, erode, or compromise the hold upon the truths held in the intellect. Furthermore, truths of the intellect are only feebly portrayed by artistic mediums sacrificing clarity—though perhaps presenting more force by stronger impression than the verbal medium. In this manner, art can provide a powerful medium for a weak message and can distort and confuse or weaken a true one. The liabilities of art undermine its strengths—or so the argument goes.

However, at this juncture, a prior and essential question is necessary about how we present these ideas. Increasingly, and historically, we have given them to the verbal medium. The reason may be that the verbal

---

14. Underhill, *Worship*, 286–87.

medium has the necessary fine structure for the enunciating and defense of truth, while art has the plasticity of subtle ambiguity and therefore the capability for distortion. But this is the admission of the power of art, even if the concession is in negative form to indict that power. Perhaps too this is an admission that art can permeate to levels of consciousness and indeed the unconscious, where it forms and stamps impressions that are difficult to vanquish, for the imagination is not only a fertile receptor (and perhaps receptive to the verbal medium least of all) but a fertile ground for thought. For this reason, we find Freud's confession that the poets had grasped his theories earlier than he, not so much a surprise as unsettling, for it evokes visions, that is to say fears, that the "authorized" modes of cognition are not in charge, though they may be in control or authority. Further, Freud's theory of psychoanalysis, so exploited by artists and the art world, was seen by many intellectuals to jeopardize the very rational character of the words we used, which were often thought of in some sense as our rationality defined. This is one reason the character of Socrates in Plato's dialogue *Ion* is so intent to show the irrationality of the poets: for if rationality does not rule the world, neither can the philosophers—and the poets have some authority. To prove the poets irrational in a rational world is to give place to the philosophers and reason.

Moreover, there may be religious suspicions cast about the beauty that may come to rest in words, for Trolestch's comment about the "unimaginative practicality" of the Reformed tradition may partially be understood as responding to the fear of what becomes of truth when the reason or conviction of the word as truth finds competition from the beauty of the word as beautiful. If the latter is deemed a lesser reason to grasp and hold onto that word of truth, then the motive for belief may generate suspicions. Perhaps even the notion of "naked truth" as a secondary layer of protection and defense of the truth is presumptuous, for truth in and of itself should be adequate, it might be argued. In other words, truth of itself should be adequate to do its own advertising. Indeed, it has no need of advertisers, or adjectives. "Naked truth" is a concept meant to fasten the argument for truth upon itself with no embellishments needed—and certainly none that resonate with the senses.

This fear may be that the prophetic word, if beautiful, may be fated to become as the amoral ritual of the ritualist, and thus is judged as having nothing to do with real and true religion; the word seen as beautiful may produce the same effect. In other words, the reason for believing may be deemed as important as the truth believed, and the reason to believe the truth should be because it is the truth and not because of enticements we wrongly attach to it, so the critic says. "Beauty" may be just such a thing.

However, one might say, as I would contend, that this is simply too much fear for truth, by insisting upon protecting the purity of truth by only allowing it to be believed for what we may deem are only the purest of reasons. It seems, however, that in this view what are elicited or requested are only the loftiest of reasons for belief to count as true belief or true religion. But this presumes to do the thinking of God for God; that is, that the human should be drawn to truth for what amounts to reasons of indifference, or, said another way, the subject should be drawn to the object for only objective reasons. However, C. S. Lewis, in his work, *The Problem of Pain*, indicates the graciousness of the Christian God in God's response to human belief coming forward for a variety of reasons—though some human inclinations of course are rather self-serving and thus not precisely the purest of reasons. They nevertheless seem acceptable and welcome by God:

> It is hardly complimentary to God that we should choose him as an alternative to hell. Yet even this he accepts. The creature's illusion of self-sufficiency must, for the creature's sake, be shattered. And by trouble, or fear of trouble on earth, by crude fear of [punishment], God shatters it, unmindful of his glory's diminution. I call this "divine humility," because it's a poor thing to strike our colours to God when the ship is going down under us, a poor thing to come to him as a last resort, to offer up our own when it is no longer worth keeping. If God were proud, he would hardly have us on such terms. But he is not proud. He stoops to conquer. He would have us even though we have shown that we prefer everything else to him, and come to him because there is nothing better now to be had.[15]

Aesthetic reasons to believe, nevertheless, are not perhaps deemed good or sufficient reasons to believe.[16] However, as applied to the Christian

---

15. Lewis, *Problem of Pain*, 97. In the same paragraph, Lewis goes on to note that what we might call the necessity of prior cleansing before coming to God, comes perilously close to a notion of self-sufficiency, which I have noted at places in this work. "If God were a Kantian, who would not have us till we came to Him from the purest and best motives, who could be saved? And this illusion of self-sufficiency may be at its strongest in some very honest, kindly, and temperate people . . ."

16. Additionally, the religious worship of the ritualist and the sacramentalist in particular may seem to look more like magic than religion. In this ascending notion, religion should look more rational than mystical or mysterious. This is largely because to the Protestant, magic is a phenomenon present in the act of unknowing, whereas real religion is embodied in the subjective grasp of objective truth. For the same reason, though

Denuded Devotion to Christ

Gospel, at even the most basic level, the "Good News" simply could not be accurately understood as simply the "News." In other words, the objection seems to mistakenly assume that belief should only present itself for what we might call objective reasons. There is much human history behind such a conception, particularly in philosophy and science. Moreover, there is a philosophical tradition running from Plato to the positivists of the twentieth century, when the obsession to guard truth from error, or to discern the same, forces truth into narrower and narrower channels. But one might say, the effect is to make it less and less attractive.[17] One could of course simply ask what attractiveness has to do with truth.

Aside from the particulars of the Christian Gospel lending it to the aesthetic exhuberance found in many Christian traditions, the aesthetic of bareness and plainness seems dubiously confident that truth is optimally discernible when it is made most apparent or most clearly presented for understanding. In fairness to this position, the argument is not that truth

---

less so because of the obvious religious as opposed to magical affinities, "mystery" too is an entity the Protestant is somewhat uncomfortable with. The discomfort arises in the Protestant in his perception that there is hardly real religion present in any act of unknowing. I think it is for this reason that Karl Barth held the view that the biblical word of revelation must be subjectively grasped before revelation can be deemed revelation.

17. The positivists in fact followed the paths of modernity as sketched by such people as Hobbes and Locke, to confine ourselves to the English. This was more or less the triumph of what many have called the mechanical philosophy over what we might bundle as "poetry." Even before the rise of any fad like "postmodernism," astute observers were noticing that something was lost in this triumph of the former over the latter. Prof. Basil Wiley, for example, wrote in England in 1934, "The statements of science, now seem to be abstractions, [and] are generally recognized to be incapable of satisfying all the complex needs of the human spirit, though they are of unimpaired serviceableness within their own field of application. For some time we have been encountering, and we have not learned to expect, a changed tone from writers who treat of the origins of modern scientific thought. Though there is no diminution in the volume of praise which is bestowed on the giants of the seventeenth century—'the century of genius'—there is no longer the old tone of expansive optimism, the glad sense of final escape from error. Though no one denies the extent of our gains, it is more often of our losses that we are now reminded." Wiley, *The Seventeenth-Century Background*, 19. Wiley, moreover, concludes his lucid study with the Romantic reaction to all of the excess of that prized century, and its successor, the 18th century: "Philosophers of earlier and of later ages, particularly those of the nineteenth century, have thought it necessary to find a place in their systems for the 'imaginative' way of approaching truth, and some have given it the very highest credentials. But seventeenth century philosophers as a whole, and Locke above all, did not feel this necessity. It has been one of the main purposes of this book to show how inevitably the whole philosophic movement of the century told against poetry, and I need not repeat here what has already been said on this subject." Wiley, 286.

be crude or be presented as blindingly as possible to evoke attention and audience. Yet, the underlying or perhaps unspoken argument may be that focus or concentration on the truth requires no extra elements or accoutrements, particularly aesthetic elements, simply because grasping the truth for what it is, or should be, is sufficient. To call or beckon for an extra player or cast from this perspective simply shows too little faith or trust in the thing believed. In other words, truth is its own best defender. One might plausibly counter that this position exhibits too much naïve trust in the capacity of the believer to forego beauty and goodness by simply grasping a truth shorn of everything but itself. Perhaps a few philosophers can forego these qualities or "extra" attributes/quiddities for the notion of truth as truth, but most require an attendant besides logical love of truth before venturing out in life only holding the hand of reason.[18]

To fix on something of a generic conception of truth, while contending that the lure of truth as truth should be sufficient to draw all men to itself seems an odd notion. From such a perspective, "Christian" truth would hold no more promise for the adjective than it would for the noun. I would contend, however, that this position has not grasped Christian truth as "Christian" truth. In the conception I am critiquing, moreover, the particulars would hardly seem to matter, as if it is somehow illicit to look behind the noun for what adjectives it is carrying. But this may be a conception of truth that is hardly Christian. Moreover, it seems that Christian truth is a beautiful story that is true, and that much of our devotedness to it is sustained by the kind of story it is. The Christian message certainly tells the truth about us as humans, and that may send us reeling for some time, but after that we are not the same anymore, but a new creature in Christ, who promises to be with us in all things.

However, the critic may continue to maintain that an adjectival description added to the noun of "truth" merely functions to attract us to the adjective, whereas the noun in itself should be sufficient to enlist that same kind of devotion, without the need for the extraneous adjective. The analogy can be made to poor fiction writing—where a weak verb may make adjectives necessary because the verb is weak.

---

18. However, I am not presuming to make a universal argument, at least not entirely. That is, I would contend that people may be different on this point—some need or religiously benefit by ritual or beauty, while others may not. I am simply trying to make an argument of justification for those who do—and not because they are spiritually "weaker."

Denuded Devotion to Christ

However, if we pause to notice that what God did in Christ he freely did, and that that means simply that he did what he did not have to do—with apologies to Anselm, in his *Cur Deus Homo*—then what he did do acquires monumental significance, simply but astoundingly, because he freely did it. Said yet another way, God was under no obligation in his act of providing for human salvation as he did. What is freely given by him acquires staggering and unbelievable significance because the gift is: 1) entirely unmerited on the part of the receiver; and 2) completely and freely given on the part of the Giver, or God. Gratitude, to put it much, much, too lightly and much, much too feebly, would be a very natural response from the recipient.

This response is because while one may endure a struggle to come to the foot of the Cross for a variety of reasons, once there, the remade Christian is able to stand his ground and withstand his circumstances simply because the experience of being rescued and redeemed is so overwhelming as to provoke new confidence in the beneficiary. The recipient can hardly comprehend the mercy of God that put him where he is, but he now knows where he is and is stronger for it. In response, the individual cannot refrain from what he is meant to do and be as a Christian. To endure torture for Christ now, as an example, is at some level endurable, and for all of the horror of it—physical torture, possibly, even to death—it simply cannot be compared to the previous life without Christ.

A truth such as this, therefore, can provoke one to exult in living in most any circumstance. This is because the promise of Christ to go with the Christian now provides sobering truth but also real gain and assurance that he who walks through the valley of most anything will not suffer abandon by God, though there be mountains or death to tread.

The problem, therefore, in suggesting that obedience to Christian "truth" should be simply because it is "true," is this: it treats very specific Christian truth as if obedience is simply a logical function of following truth. But truth is never "naked" like this. It always comes with a covering or clothes. More particularly, the appeal to a religious "naked truth" ignores the particular and peculiar nature of the Christian truth just enunciated. Moreover, we do not treat "truth" generically, but specifically, and a wide array of examples could show this. In other words, I will respond differently to different truths simply because they are different. Furthermore, if the moral duty to truth as truth trumps all other facts to consider, we are in the methodology of the philosopher again, but this time camping with the philosopher's notion of truth conceived as a "ruthless task-master." With presumed logical knots tying up the question of the sufficiency of truth as truth, we might simply or even naively ask whether Christian redemption is a good or bad truth, a beautiful or a ghastly truth. Said another way, we cannot simply follow "correct" for truth, for then we would fall into the scholar's penchant for truth as correctness. That certainly would be a step in the right or correct direction, but hardly all of the destination.

The Aesthetic and Truth

One particular point of debate among religious reformers regarding true religion concerns the culpability of using aesthetic means to understand and appropriate the Christian message. This is especially the case for the Protestant Reformers discussed in these pages, simply because they inherited the luxuriant and overwhelming Catholic aesthetic, which was severely judged by many of them as not only unnecessarily weighty, but bringing two things together that could be separated without impoverishing the human grasp of the Christian Gospel. The historical conflict over Christian truth and the aesthetic has been succinctly depicted by Mary Warnock:

> The Church has within it a tendency to write off the aesthetic as productive not of truth but of pleasure, as frivolous therefore and a distraction from the supposedly clear question whether or not what the Church teaches is true. No one's life was ever changed, it is argued, by the beautiful. If we treat Christianity as an object of the aesthetic imagination, we treat it as a myth; we overlook the harsh realities of the moral. In accordance with arguments of this kind there have been repeated attempts in the history of the church to cut out the aesthetic from the centre of worship and return to the facts. Christianity, it is argued, must be rendered intelligible and plain, poetry and music must be banished, unless they can somehow be shown to be a necessary vehicle for the historic truth or the moral message.[19]

Many Christians undoubtedly feel the strain of such a vexing debate whereby the individual may be forced to choose between truth and beauty. This seems, too, the most basic implication of truth perceived as a kind of "naked truth." However, I have been contending that Christian truth cannot be subsumed and guarded under this hardly inviting conception of truth, for philosophers are sometimes also heard to say, while correctness is a

---

19. Warnock, "Imagination," 364–65.

necessary requirement for our notion of truth, it alone is not sufficient. My argument is that the notion of correct, though necessary, is alone insufficient as a full account of Christian truth, and that it also wrongly presumes to treat the Christian as a state of life requiring no aesthetic or material component for this truth, or, also, as being a mind with a life, but with no senses attached. This is partly and again because Christ did not come in the form of logic, but in the form and reality of a material man sent by God as God to redeem the world of men.

Nevertheless, the strain and pain and even possible death entailed in devotion to truth, can rightly make one suspicious of an aesthetic that may of course appear to have the ability or power to impoverish our ability to hold fast to the truth—much as the quotation from Warnock points out. Understandable, therefore, are the justifications offered and sometimes encouraged for pushing religious devotion and piety away from the aesthetic element because they may be regarded as ultimately extraneous luxuries competing with the hard truth of the Gospel. I am arguing that the nature of the Gospel Truth is compelling as more than simply being generically and thus blandly correct, given the nature and specifics of that truth. Nevertheless, and as an example of the complexity of this issue as it must be built around the tumult of real life, Tertullian's famous statement that the blood of the martyrs is the seed of the church might shockingly but also truthfully suggest that the most productive feature of the faith is a river of blood. The statement is indeed a striking reminder that unwanted afflictions often seem to hone a man more than his desired comforts. About this, few can dispute, for there is much Christian history from which to contend that duress and persecution often have produced spiritual health, whereas health unwisely managed can trickle down to or even run to its opposite, both in individuals and whole cultures.[20]

However, we may ask the question in another and I think better way: When one is under the siege of afflictions, to what does he turn, lacking his usual comforts and perhaps well-nigh everything else? With reference to this question, and to emphasize that we are not considering a mere hypothetical question, we might turn to a passage from Boethius's famous work, *The Consolation of Philosophy*, where the accused Boethius is languishing in prison awaiting execution, but with two competing consolers at his feet. Boethius had been accused of treason, but in better days, he had been a

---

20. This is a frequent estimation of what happened to the spiritual state of the church after Constantine as a result of the conversion of that emperor to the Christian religion.

gifted philosopher, though his desire for comfort in his plight has led him to consider other comforters. It is in this situation that Boethius, the pitiable prisoner awaiting death, confronts his weaknesses. The consoler Lady Philosophy appears to him and severely chastises Boethius for giving audience to her competing though weaker rival, namely, poetry. In his account of her severe rebuke to her languishing and withering student, Boethius writes,

> When she saw the Muses of poetry standing beside my bed and consoling me with their words, she was momentarily upset and glared at them with burning eyes. 'Who let these whores from the theater come to the bedside of this sick man?' she said. 'They cannot offer medicine for his sorrows; they will nourish him only with their sweet poison. They kill the fruitful harvest of reason with the sterile thorns of the passions; they do not liberate the minds of men from disease, but merely accustom them to it. I would find it easier to bear if your flattery had, as it usually does, seduced some ordinary dull-witted man; in that case, it would have been no concern of mine. But this man has been educated in the philosophical schools of the Eleatics and the Academy. Get out Sirens; your sweetness leads to death. Leave him to be cured and made strong by my Muses.[21]

To abide with Lady Philosophy's advice of rebuke requires an allegiance to reason so as to effectively resist the solicitous senses, something that, as Lady Philosophy seems to suggest, could not be expected of the masses. More is expected of Boethius, however, for he is a philosopher and one with a good education and knowledge at his back, and an individual more than adequate to face down his future. However, this advice, historically considered, could end in troubles of another sort, as the later medieval scholastic in centuries after Boethius would be accused of doing. In other words, their rationalism swallows their religion, as Bernard of Clairvaux would claim. Lady Philosophy charges, however, in the case of Boethius, that he has allowed the poet in him or the love and consolation of poetry, to swallow or trump the philosopher in him.

The human condition having been visited in miniature, we return to our question of what humans need or require so as to expediate their Christian devotion, or practice of true religion. That is, is Lady Philosophy missing something or requiring something too difficult or foreign for her

---

21. Boethius, *The Consolation of Philosophy*, 2–3.

frail listener, as she dismisses the muses of poetry for the heady fount of philosophy? Furthermore, is her advice for her philosophy student applicable to the non-philosophers among us, both in and out of prison?

Friedrich Nietzsche, though of course and notoriously not a religious believer, ventured the suggestion that the vitality of a religion or its capacity to sustain believers wanes when the mythos of a religion is lanced for the sake of what I have termed "naked truth." What happens is that there becomes an insistence on belief as true, though not simply because this is all the reason that is necessary for belief, but because the belief, in coming under attack, may feel the need to shed "extraneous" components for survival. With some exaggerations, Nietzsche makes his point this way:

> For this is the way in which religions are wont to die out: when under the stern, intelligent eyes of an orthodox dogmatism, the mythical premises of a religion are systematized as a sum total of historical events; when one begins apprehensively to defend the credibility of the myths, while at the same time one opposes any continuation of their natural vitality and growth; when, accordingly the feeling for myth perishes, and its place is taken by the claim of religion to historical foundations.[22]

We might, as similar too, reference Oscar Wilde's contention that religions die when they are proved true. However, with such contentions and despite the exaggerations, the point being made of course is not that truth kills, but rather that certain conceptions of truth may diminish the capacity of that truth to draw or hold its adherents. Nietzsche's point seems considerable to me. Moreover, I think his description describes something akin to what is often characterized simply as dead orthodoxy, but not of the usual variety. This will be an orthodoxy that retreats to concepts over content, but more of that later.

Nietzsche's point is that the life of a religion that retreats scarcely allows growth. Nietzsche seems to think that something like fear of error, for example, almost necessarily provokes the adherents to maintain only the deemed essentials. A reductionism may be the result. We might speculate that part of the real vitality of religious life and devotion comes with a time when the religion was closer to life—and perhaps closer to content than concepts formed from it, whereas in time, the religion may bend life for a concept not really found in the content. So, whereas life may have provided

---

22. Nietzsche, *Birth of Tragedy*, 68.

occasion for our conception of the world to be reworked, such as by the Incarnation, the conceptual outworking of the new idea may turn to impinge upon that which came into the world, so that the concept grows away from the content. One might make the point in the manner of Josef Pieper with his reference to the Incarnation: "The step from Thales to Socrates, or from Plato to the Stoa, cannot be compared with the step from Thales, Socrates, Plato, and the Stoa on one hand, to Origen, Augustine, Anselm, and Thomas on the other hand. For in the latter case a particular event intervened between the two epochs—an event not in the realm of ideas and concepts, but in the historical realm; not in the sphere of definitions of reality, but in the sphere of reality itself."[23]

However, one may systemize and philosophize religious faith away from life, while paradoxically claiming the reverse. In other words, Christianity unquestionably came into the world with the Incarnation, but devotees may seek to maintain themselves in abstention from this event, for various, but hardly good reasons. An unorthodox Christian theological perspective may indeed deny the whole inconceivable event because it is deemed inconceivable, but orthodox traditions may affirm it while neglecting it to the point of negating it, out of the fear of the allied sensual or material liabilities outweighing the assets. Thus, much of the life of religious devotion as coming to terms with the God who became man will be a cognitive affair, largely shorn of the senses.

In many ways, Protestantism put the Christian religion closer to humans, but in other ways, it went the way of the philosophers, by inadvertently or unintentionally pushing content and context away from the concept, until arriving at the naked truth, shorn of everything but itself, as the "naked Christ," corresponding to little but itself as a concept conveying little. That is, we might make this point in an example, a period of history when the elucidated concept starts to displace the realism of the story, such that the concept displaces the things that came, much as Hegel will argue for the desired philosophical consciousness that can think beyond "things." What gave life to the religion through its stories and history is subsumed to serve the underlying theological framework lifted from the former, and one starts to try to live off the latter, without benefit of the former. However, one may in time feel famished for doing so, though paradoxically after having moved to a higher level of consciousness, as in Hegel, or "true religion," as with the early Reformed thinkers.

23. Pieper, *Scholasticism*, 17.

Denuded Devotion to Christ

As an example of this, in talking to a Christian friend some time ago, I told him something that I think most people would concede—that a story has an appeal to a reader or listener that an outline or map or chart does not, and that therefore it was a mistake to trump the great stories of the Bible in too much haste to discover the underlying theology, whereby the stories are left behind or relegated to being appendages or husks, whereas the story supplied the point from which the story is made in the beginning. He expressed agreement with the point, but went on to say that in his theological training, he had been trained otherwise. That is, he had received training in the form of a theological outline with proof texts attached. The natural love of the story was trumped one might say for the point of the story, which would in time turn into a concept.

In this manner, however, my friend was trained and schooled like a philosopher—that is, to catch or comprehend the essential point, and thus, though surely most unconsciously, to relegate the rest to a kind of context or periphery, though the "periphery" provided the point to begin with, and is somewhat analogous to Pieper's point about the Incarnation, and will be my contention about history in the final chapter.

Much of this issue, that is, the need to enlist the senses in Christian religious devotion comes back to how we learn, but remembering also that our senses have been disciplined in the critiqued conception talked about in this book. But if we are capable of learning something from a story that we cannot from an outline or grid, we might ask if any room is left for the concept or conceptualization and the philosopher, whom I have treated fairly critically in these pages. However, the question I have in mind is asked by Robert C. Roberts:

> If we have narrative displays of the virtues, what good are philosophical ones to us? Why not just read Sophocles and leave Aristotle on the shelf? Why read *Either/Or* when we have *Middlemarch*? The answer, I think, is that we human beings come to understand in a variety of ways, which are mutually supplementary. We would never get any very adequate understanding of Paris by sitting in our hotel room exploring the *Plan Taride*. But without such a map (or at least one that we construct for ourselves from a great deal of ground-level exploring) we would not know as well where we are in our ramblings about Paris. The map is a more abstract, schematic representation of the very same Paris that we see and hear and smell as we walk along the Seine or wander the markets and neighborhood streets of some out-of-the-way arrondissement.

> Philosophers from Plato to Wittgenstein have felt that to understand is somehow to display the essence of whatever it is they were trying to understand.[24]

This author is justifying philosophy as a sort of needed and useful distillation from the complexity of our experience of the world. That is, like the road map of which he speaks, it makes more coherent the many bits and pieces of our experience. It is, at the same time, however, more abstract, and though it may tell you things about the "world" it depicts, there are things about that world that the map reduces to fit itself. Therefore, the map in his example is not all there is to Paris and certainly not Paris. This is a shortcoming of the map, but Paris without a map, except to the very few, is less intelligible. Philosophy is certainly not everything, and maybe not even the best of all things, but like the map, it is a help and helps us order our lives and get around. However, conceptual knowledge abstaining from sensual acquaintances may squander significant opportunities for acquaintance.

Part of the problem of philosophy is its directness, for in cutting past the meat to get to the marrow of naked truth, it leaves out a lot—and thus in its own way, may loosen or weaken our dedication to truth, in the way that Nietzsche suggests. This, moreover, was precisely the fear of the aesthetic that we earlier addressed. Nevertheless, our criticism may venture to respond to Lady Philosophy that rationalism does not consist of the whole human, but rather only a part. In D. H. Lawrence's essay, "Why the Novel Matters," he portrays the selectivity, but also perhaps the assumption of the philosopher as well as the saint and the scientist on this question:

> And as for the sum of all knowledge, it can't be anything more than an accumulation of all the things I know in the body, and you, dear reader, know in the body. These damned philosophers, they talk as if they suddenly went off in steam, and were then much more important than they are when they're in their shirts. It is nonsense. Every man, philosopher included, ends in his own finger tips . . . It seems impossible to get a saint, or a philosopher, or a scientist, to stick to this simple truth. They are all, in a sense, renegades. The saint wishes to offer himself up as spiritual food for the multitude . . . The philosopher, on the other hand, because he can think, decides that nothing but thoughts matter. It is as if a rabbit, because he can make little pills, should decide that nothing but little pills matter. As for the scientist, he has absolutely no use for me so long

---

24. Roberts, "Narrative Ethics," 477–78.

Denuded Devotion to Christ

as I am man alive. To the scientist, I am dead. He puts under the microscope a bit of dead me, and calls it me.[25]

As we will note in the final chapter, my friend's story about biblical stories and theological points is somewhat analogous to the way Hegel treats history: where religious materialism turns into philosophical systems, shedding matter. But people for the most part do not live their lives nor direct their interests that way, nor, I would venture, think all their thoughts that way. However, under the assault on the material side of Christian devotion, Christian lives may take another form of life as the proverbial philosopher who is critically minded enough to not need a story—maybe not even, if he cares to think about it—The Greatest Story Ever Told.

---

25. Lawrence, "Why the Novel Matters," 83–84.

True Religion and the Philosophical Consciousness

Displacement of Materiality in the Practice of True Religion

IN HEGEL'S ESTIMATION, THE TRANSITION FROM RELIGIOUS TO PHILOSOPHical consciousness is not inevitable, but offers the real possibility of moving beyond the historical association of the religious mind that remains tagged with temporalness and material being. For Hegel, humankind advances in self-knowledge with the philosophical consciousness as a progression from successive and prior states of cultural consciousness. Nietzsche, in bold contrast to Hegel, characterizes the chief error of the philosophers as this flight from temporalness and the material world. The presumed superior knowledge of the rational philosopher's dream of a philosophical consciousness loosed from indebtedness to the material world is for Nietzsche a regression. Disagreeing with Hegel's judgment on materiality, Nietzsche criticizes that judgment as an identifying trait of the philosophers. It is for Nietzsche one of the fundamental errors of the philosophers. It is shared in the conception of "true religion," as that conception moves Christian devotion closer to the philosophers.

The evaluation of materiality among rationalist philosophers, such as Hegel, therefore, contrasts sharply to philosophers not in that rational tradition, such as Nietzsche. Furthermore, in comparison to Hegel's cultural succession of art, religion and philosophy, in Nietzsche's conception, humankind rises above religion, science, and philosophy, to art. This contrast provides for more differences between Nietzsche and Hegel that resonate from their respective difference over the place of materiality in life and culture. Because of this difference, when they come to Christianity, we find

Hegel in sympathy with Protestantism and despising Catholicism, whereas Nietzsche detests Protestantism in his preference for Catholicism and prefers the Old Testament over the New. Hegel, on the other hand, clearly prefers the New Testament to the Old, and like many Reformed thinkers, is fond of quoting from the Gospel of John to theologically vindicate his spiritualistic view of religious advancement. As might be expected, many of the things Hegel most despises in Catholicism are the same things Nietzsche treasures. Though disagreeing about the propriety of sensuality and materiality, they nonetheless agree in it largely not belonging to philosophy, Hegel prescriptively so, while Nietzsche denounces the desire for separation from the material world that has historically characterized philosophers.

The specific element of the realization of rationalism that I have focused upon in the Reformed tradition is the diminution of sensuality or the material element and the corresponding and inevitable accentuation on the mind within that tradition. Thus, though the Reformed thinkers are religious reformers seeking to expunge philosophy from theology, on another level, they make possible the philosophical consciousness inside their religious tradition by their impugning of materiality in religious devotion and practice. In a word, as Hegel describes the process, the philosophical consciousness begins to look past the preceding but confining embodiment of religious objects and practices, to a human consciousness resonating with the Mind of God.

As an example of this within the Reformation tradition, the contention of Zwingli seems to imply that commensurability between spirits as spirits provides a required platform for the relation between God and humans. This specification for religious commensurability is in vivid contrast to the overtly religious unlikeness between God and humans laid down by other Reformers such as Martin Luther. For Luther the problem of incommensurability between God and humans was an issue, though it was not incommensurability of matter to spirit, but rather of a righteous God to sinful humans. Zwingli's conception of the relationship to God seems built on an underlying metaphysical identity between God and humans. Whereas in medieval Catholicism that identity had in part presented itself in terms of sacramentalism—and thus the lush expression of material devotion—in Zwingli the relation is found in spirit to spirit, or, in Zwingli's revealing words of interchange—mind. Relationship with God seems to follow from the mode of the being of God. The point hardly seems religious in itself, though perhaps akin to some forms of natural religion. Nevertheless, metaphysical congruity seems requisite to Divine-human engagement for Zwingli.

This kind of "fit," however, pushes the body of the finite worshipper, as one example, to the periphery, along with the diminution of other material objects and practices of religious devotion. With God conceived of as essentially transcendent, the Christ of the Incarnation, though a physical being, is nevertheless escalated into a metaphysical being; metaphysics takes precedence over physics—so too for the human. Having shorn God and the human person of most things but spirit for religious devotion, that is to say mind, emphasis will now by default almost necessarily fall upon thinking, with little value placed on sensing. Thus, the emphasis upon personal religion, coupled with the reticence toward tangible and material devotional aids, forces religious devotion to work almost solely from the head.[1] This is the general manner in which experience and rationalism couple in this conception of true religion.[2]

The work of the philosophical consciousness is justified in Hegel as necessary for humanity in the interest of expanding a religious knowledge restricted by the form of material representation. This is similar to the Reformed tradition's notion of true religion, for this perspective largely attributes the errors of false religion to the material components and practices of false religion. For Hegel, the progressive diminution of the "things" of

---

1. One estimate of this comes from Margaret Miles: "The problem of formulating a description of the relationship of mind and body which adequately accounts for both experiential data and the requirements of systematic thought is the decisive problem of human thought; a changed description requires fundamental and painful reorientations of energy and value. The stone which the classical builders had rejected in their conceptual edifice was the body; but, in the manner which Freud has elucidated for us, a denial is simultaneously an affirmation, a focus which gives the lie to its intellectual negation and evidences itself psychologically as ambivalence, frustration, and eventually sterility in thought and action." Miles, *Augustine*, 1.

2. To my mind the history of the fate of the Reformed Puritan experience is a result of its diminution of all other sensibilities, save the cognitive, from religious experience. Thus, the Reformed notion of religious experience founders on the cognitivism in which one tries to live more or less in a Romantic world but insists that devotional life be lived on Rationalistic premises. The "heart," though important in Puritanism, cannot be fed in the Puritan experience, because even though the Puritan lived in his heart, he tried, or only allowed his heart to be fed from his head and logic, and not from his feelings. Alan Simpson makes the point that "The whole history of Puritanism is a commentary on its failure to satisfy the cravings which its preaching had aroused." Simpson, *Puritanism*, 28. Eugene White has written of Puritanism, that "Its tragic flaw was the issue of emotion in religion. Its chief legacy may be the continuing conflict between emotion and reason." White, *Puritan Rhetoric*, 64.

Denuded Devotion to Christ

religion by the philosophical consciousness disciplines a religious consciousness awash in material aids, objects, and practices and antiquated history. In Hegel's view, religious consciousness imbibes a sensual form that inhibits and delays higher knowledge until the material components of that religious mentality are seen through by the philosophical consciousness. In the move from religious consciousness, however, Hegel claims not a philosophical rewriting or reconstruction of the Christian religion, but instead that consciousness moves thought to a form where knowledge, pinned down before now, advances. It does so, Hegel contends, without losing or cancelling those aspects of religion not shackled to the limiting material form of the religious consciousness.[3] Forms of "partial" knowing, however, such as the material representations and crosses of art and faith, can hardly be regarded with finality, though the religious consciousness, left to itself and steeped in material things, can indefinitely confine and strap that consciousness to the constraints of the material elements represented. In other words, rather than progression, there can be stagnation of the Spirit or Mind.

Hegel judges the fate of Catholic religious practice this way. Some of the early Protestant Reformers seem to reflect something of the same judgment. Given the compliant nature of Catholicism to the material elements of Christianity, the Catholic consciousness lies shackled to a church focused on the material markers as the makers of religious faith.

In the history and story of Jesus—the historical babe, youngster in the temple, teacher-rabbi, crucified person—such events chronicle the life of Christ, but can blind the devotee to the underlying and escalated transcendence. What one concentrates on reflects the consciousness in charge. Consideration of the divinity of Christ, moreover, calls forth the work of a philosophically inclined consciousness to consider the metaphysical significance of the historical person, though Jesus remains by and large as the material Galilean in Catholic forms of piety according to Hegel.

Lawrence Stepelevich has commented on how Hegel configures this progression of thought using the Incarnation as example: "But yet this long-awaited reconciliation has its negative side, for God, although present in the world as actual subject, is yet an exclusive, sensible presence. Divinity cannot be communicated to all in *this* particular form. The Incarnation

---

3. Hegel's broader view of Spirit coming to intellectual culmination can be seen as respective forms of knowing culminating in the philosophical (and therefore the highest) knowledge of God, which, in Hegel's mind, turns out to be knowledge of the self.

True Religion and the Philosophical Consciousness

must be annulled in its finite aspects, and the limiting flesh must be dissolved so that the ideal of divinity can be present to all for all time . . . It is therefore requisite that the particular physicality of Jesus be reconciled with the universality of the abstract God . . ."[4]

In this manner, the Incarnation, though necessary to initiate knowledge of and to affirm the transcendent Spirit, at the same time presents and presides in a material and finite form that can only extend so far. That limitation is not only physical, but also historical according to Hegel. There must be an extension beyond the simple physical event of the Incarnation, and more importantly, to the "universality of the abstract God." Were the person of Jesus to remain only as a material image clothed and stapled and stitched in the religious mind and culture as an object, then He would remain in the form of the crucifix and the icon, with the historical Jesus embodied, but also embalmed, in that history. For Hegel, however, the Jesus who became local must go universal. Temporal historical presence is significant, except the attachment to the historical dimension can lapse into bondage to the historical figure shown in the materialistic worship of Catholicism. That devotion for Hegel hardly hints at the God or Spirit of transcendence or universality.[5]

Hegel's notion of the subservience of history here is noteworthy, especially as he seems to convey that history serves as a husk, a servant to something greater, and as an instalment that is eventually rolled back or peeled away for the underlying idea brought to consummation by philosophical comprehension. For Hegel, history provides the content that takes the growing mind to the expansive philosophical consciousness where history will eventually be left behind. History reminds us of contingency, but through it thought protrudes with eternity. In this way and not only in Hegel but Kant[6] also, one witnesses the role of history serving reason. Stepelvich has correctly concluded with reference to Hegel,

---

4. Stepelvich, "Hegel and the Lutheran Eucharist," 270.

5. Hegel oddly seems not to conceive that a God lifted and abstracted from the resonances of material being with human beings might be elusive.

6. Kant, for example, in his *Religion within the Limits of Reason Alone*, 102, writes, "The Mohammedans know very well how to ascribe a spiritual meaning to the description of their paradise, which is dedicated to sensuality of every kind; the Indians do exactly the same thing in their interpretation of their Vedas, at least for the enlightened portion of their people. That this can be done without ever and again offending greatly against the literal meaning of the popular faith is due to the fact that, earlier by far than this faith, the predisposition to the moral religion lay hidden in human reason; and though its first rude manifestations took the form merely of practices of divine worship,

> And so, what is philosophically, i.e. really, occurring in history is mental activity, the subsuming of all temporal events and experienced objectivity into the one overreaching consciousness of Absolute Knowledge. History is the act and the record of the victory of spirit over matter, of intention over extension. The reported history of the religious consciousness is mired in imagery, and thus unable to present a fully rational explanation but only a "miraculous"—i.e., unnatural/supernatural—explanation of what has happened and will happen.[7]

In the case of Hegel, history provides the truth emerging from the long and arduous road of human history. That is, though history is initially required as an expedient for the entry of reason or transcendence, it nevertheless comes in the front door not as an occupant-owner, but as a guest. Thus, it leaves as it came, its purpose served and its presence momentary in a house that can now maintain itself in the absence of its former guest—though the visit was necessary. In this way, history, as the province of the sensible and the particular, is indeed temporary, but nevertheless has importance as the carrier of something higher than itself. For this reason, the material of history must be dispatched but also disciplined by the progressive management of reason. History has served its purpose in another, just as religion has too, for both are consummated in philosophical understanding that initially required them.

It is of course one thing to ascribe such a view of history to Hegel or professional philosophers; it is another to intimate that the Protestant Reformed tradition in some manner like Hegel is precariously balancing and perhaps finally imprisoning history in the slighting of the sensible.

---

and for this very purpose gave rise to those alleged revelations, yet these manifestations have infused even into the myths, though unintentionally, something from the nature of their supersensible origin. Nor can we charge such interpretations with dishonesty, provided we are not disposed to assert that the meaning which we ascribe to the symbols of the popular faith, even to the holy books, is exactly as intended by them, but rather allow this question to be left undecided and merely admit the *possibility* that their authors may be so understood. For the final purpose even of reading these holy scriptures, or of investigating their content, is to make men better; the historical element, which contributes nothing to this end, is something which is in itself quite indifferent, and we can do with it what we like. Historical faith 'is dead, being alone'; that is, of itself, regarded as a creed, it contains nothing, and leads to nothing, which could have any moral value for us."

7. Stepelvich, "Hegel and the Lutheran Eucharist," 267.

However, if history is the carrier of the sensible particular, the attitude toward one might not be unrelated to the attitude toward the other.[8]

Such a suggestion may appear particularly outrageous on two specific points, as it relates to Protestantism at the time of the Reformation. One is the well-known Reformation insistence on an historical and grammatical method of scriptural interpretation as opposed to the perceived fanciful allegorical and four-fold method commonly employed in the Middle Ages. An insistence on the former in particular would certainly seem to evidence great deference to history. The other consideration is the traditional theological staple that in Protestantism it is in fact in human history, and not so much in nature (as in Catholicism, or at least more so in Catholicism) that the activity or revelation of God is exhibited and therefore most upheld. This difference seems in great part to show up in Protestant hesitation toward the Catholic appetite for sacramentalism. Therefore, given these Protestant distinctives, it is also instructive that on the issue of the appropriateness of the material element in worship, Reformed argument is largely positioned in defense of the transcendence of God. We have noted, however, but relatedly, Luther's resistance to the spiritualizing tendency of Karlstadt and Zwingli. Yet Hegel, who seems much nearer to Karlstadt and Zwingli than to Luther on this issue, proclaims himself proudly a Lutheran.[9]

Moreover, in Hegel's claim to align the philosophical consciousness as emerging from within Protestantism, Hegel clearly intended his description of Lutheranism to specially serve or at least accommodate his own philosophy. Catholic religious practice, by contrast, was mired in "things," at the price of subservient human subjects. In Hegel's *Philosophy of Religion* he writes:

> [In Catholicism] God is thus known as something external in the Lord's Supper—this midpoint of doctrine—this externality is the foundation of the whole Catholic religion. Thus arises the servitude of knowledge and activity; this externality pervades all

---

8. Luxon, *Literal Figures*, 82, has argued that particularly in the case of the Reformed thinkers, the effort to make God and Christ supersensible and transcendent "had the effect of denying the historical any claim to reality."

9. Hegel, *Lectures on the History of Philosophy*, Vol. I: 73. On this point Stepelvich in "Hegel and the Lutheran Eucharist," 269, contends, "despite the *prima facie* case that can be made for Hegel's Lutheranism by reason of his own direct and presumably honest declarations to that effect, Hegel actually viewed Lutheranism, and particularly its Eucharistic doctrine, as but an imperfect prefiguration of his own philosophy, which was intended—as Hegelian thought was assimilated—to finally and totally replace Lutheranism."

further characteristics since the true is represented as something fixed and eternal. *As something existing outside the subject*, it can pass into the control of others; the church is in possession of it as well as of all the means of grace. In every respect the subject is a passive, receptive subject that knows not what is true, right, and good, but has to accept the standard from others. (Italics mine)[10]

We see here Hegel's condemnation of what he regards as the excessive "objectivity" of Catholic religious doctrine and practice. Hegel's repugnance for the Catholic conception stems from his dislike of an objectivity not yielding to something akin to a form of modern subjectivity. For here is a subject still governed by other subjects much like Kant's famous description of Enlightenment arising out of rejection of a self-incurred tutelage or subservience to another. Worse, however, for Hegel is for a human subject to submit to religious belief for reason of something outside of himself, as Hegel perceived does the Catholic devotee to the Eucharist. Thus, Stepelvich rightly says that "the doctrine of transubstantiation represents a view that is deeply opposed to the ambitions of his system."[11] Comparing Hegel's criticism of the Catholic view to Lutheranism on the same point, we find the following statement from Hegel:

> The relation of Spirit to itself alone is the absolute determination; the divine spirit lives in its own communion and presence. This comprehension has been called Faith, but it is not an historical faith; we Lutherans—I am a Lutheran and will remain the same—have only this original faith. The Supper is, according to the Lutheran conception, of Faith alone; it is a divine satisfaction, and is not adored as if it were the Host. Thus a sacred image is no more to us than is a stone or thing. The second point of view (the historical) must indeed be that with which consciousness begins; it must start from the external comprehension of this form . . . But if it remain where it is, that is the unspiritual point of view: to remain fixed in this second standpoint in the dead far-away historic distance, is to reject the Spirit.[12]

Though Catholics are not mentioned by name here, we can see Hegel's jab at the material components and vehicles of worship in Catholic religious practice. Also notable is that Hegel hardly gives a correct view of the Lutheran position on the "Supper." Luther most certainly did not regard the

---

10. Hegel, *Lectures on the Philosophy of Religion*, Vol. III: 338.
11. Stepelvich, "Hegel and the Lutheran Eucharist," 264.
12. Hegel, *Lectures on the History of Philosophy*, Vol. I: 73.

elements of the Eucharist as "no more to us than is a stone or thing," though perhaps Hegel did. This characterization is more fitting of Zwingli's view. Still yet to be noticed is Hegel's linking of what amounts to the Catholic view to the "dead far-away historic distance" and externality. Thus, while conceding the necessity of the historical for the religious consciousness, it is nevertheless a transient consciousness for Hegel. Perhaps even more revealing of Hegel's own position and its deviation from Lutheranism is what he has to say concerning the Reformed view of the Eucharist. It is criticized by Hegel as "a memorial, an ordinary psychological relation; everything speculative has disappeared, being annulled in the relations of the community. The Reformed Church is therefore the place where divinity and truth collapse into the prose of the Enlightenment and of mere understanding, and in the contingency of subjective particularity."[13]

As has been observed by others, Hegel has more accurately depicted the Zwinglian rather than the Calvinist view here.[14] Nevertheless, Hegel's criticism of the Reformed view is the opposite of that levelled at the Catholic view.[15] In Hegel's estimation, the Reformed view succumbs to an excess subjectivity.[16]

However, Hegel does claim that with the *Christian* religion, the unique characteristics needed to give rise to philosophical conception out of religious form are present[17] because the transition from the religious to the

13. Hegel, *Lectures on the Philosophy of Religion*, Vol. III: 272.

14. Westphal in *Hegel*, 89, writes that "He [Hegel] evidently has the Zwinglian view in mind rather than the Calvinist, which retains the concept of real presence." Stepelvich in "Hegel and the Lutheran Eucharist," 271–72, speculates that "It is of interest to note that Hegel's 'Reformed Church' is identified only with that following the teaching of Ulrich Zwingli, and not that of the Calvinist confession. This neglect of a major confession may have been deliberately chosen, if only for the sake of dialectical tidiness, as the introduction of a *fourth* Eucharistic doctrine would be incommensurate with Hegel's usual triadic expressions."

15. In some sense, Hegel sees the Catholic and Reformed view on opposite ends of the spectrum in terms of the relation of object to subject. He of course thinks the Lutheran view, informed by his philosophy, weds the two. However, as I have said above, his view is much closer to Zwingli than to Luther.

16. In my view, Hegel for the most part gives an accurate assessment of the failings of the Zwingli, though they are also criticisms I would to a great degree charge to Hegel's own philosophical system. This is in part because in Hegel's philosophical idealism, in a sense, the subject becomes the object and objective world.

17. However, my purpose in this chapter is not to attempt to unite Hegel and the Reformed thinkers as bearing out the ultimate philosophical nature or adjudication of Christianity, nor is the resemblance of some of Hegel's views compared to the Reformed thinkers' evidence that Hegel was Reformed.

Denuded Devotion to Christ

philosophical consciousness requires the right kind of seed to germinate and grow into philosophical consciousness. This progress of consciousness occurs as true religion carries the resources required for the next step and finds consummation in philosophy. What is retained in the shift of consciousness between the two is not so much religion as it is the truth of religion. The truth of religion is ultimately not resident in its material objects, and not in the embedded idea, for in Hegel's mind, religion arrives in a husk of history and materiality that philosophy pierces through to the uncloaked and then released idea. In this event, philosophy does not bring to religious consciousness a new content, but it does bring a new form and a new understanding to religion. The truth of religion, explicated and understood by the philosophical consciousness, represents a truth that transcends the specific and sensual component of the religious consciousness. This is not to say, moreover, that the rise of conceptualization out of philosophical consciousness in Hegel's system signals the demise of religion, along with art—the prior movements of spirit in Hegel's philosophical system. Rather, it is the case for Hegel, that "Art and religion are the modes in which the Absolute Idea is present for non-philosophical people, creatures of feeling, perceptions, pictorial thinking."[18] Thus, Hegel demarcates between religion and philosophy on the basis of a comparison between the conceptualization of philosophy as contrasted to the pictorial thinking and feeling belonging to art and to religion. In Hegel's mind, religion pictures or represents the Absolute, while philosophy, as a higher movement, conceives or thinks the Absolute. It is nevertheless the case for Hegel that the same truth is expressed by religion and philosophy, for he says in *Introduction to the Lectures on the History of Philosophy*, "But, strictly speaking, philosophy's topic is God alone, or its aim is to know God. This topic it has in common with religion but with this difference, namely that religion treats the subject pictorially while philosophy thinks and comprehends it."[19]

---

18. Hegel, *Introduction to the Lectures on the History of Philosophy*, 28.

19. Ibid., 62. Hegel also writes in his *Encyclopaedia Logic*, 24, "It is true that it [philosophy] does, initially, have its objects in common with religion. Both of them have the *truth* in the highest sense of the word as their object, for both hold that *God* and God *alone* is the truth." In his *Philosophy of Mind*, 302–3, Hegel explains that "Here might seem to be the place to treat in a definite exposition of the reciprocal relations of philosophy and religion. The whole question turns entirely on the difference of the forms of speculative thought from the forms of mental representation and 'reflecting' intellect . . . It is only by an insight into the value of these forms that the true and needful conviction can be gained, that the content of religion and philosophy is the same . . ."

True Religion and the Philosophical Consciousness

Thus, religion and philosophy are not talking about different things; rather, they are talking about virtually the same things differently. In Hegel's mind, while there is some equivalence of subject matter, there is an expression of knowledge rising to the ultimate conceptions of philosophical comprehension. The conceptualization of philosophy, therefore, exceeds but also had previous need of religious consciousness because religious consciousness points to and makes possible the philosophical consciousness. Thus, philosophy depicts the rationale of religion, but in so doing, philosophy as conceptualization shows its superior position: "This science [Philosophy] is the unity of Art and Religion. Whereas the vision-method of Art, external in point of form, is but subjective production and shivers the substantial content into many separate shapes and whereas Religion, with its separation into parts, opens it out in mental picture, and mediates what is thus opened out; Philosophy not merely keeps them together to make a total, but even unifies them into the simple spiritual vision, and then in that raises them to self-conscious thought."[20]

Philosophy, therefore, in this description, presupposes a content upon which it conceptualizes. But also to be noticed is Hegel's contention that religion produces a "mental picture." This mental picture provides and provokes the first steps toward the actual advance of self-conscious thought, as away from the purely sensible form, from which the representations of religion arise. The representation is by its very nature symbolic of the mind; thus, in the mental pictures of religion produced in the religious consciousness are the first stirrings of the philosophical consciousness. As already indicated, philosophy and conceptualization are not enterprises that begin with themselves because "Philosophy lacks the advantage, which the other sciences enjoy, of being able to *presuppose* its *ob-jects* as given immediately by representation . . . The reason is that in the order of time consciousness produces *representations* of ob-jects before it produces concepts of them; and that the *thinking* spirit only advances to thinking cognition and comprehension by going *through* representation and by converting itself *to* it."[21]

Philosophy, therefore, is parasitic upon its host, religion, but in the progression of religious consciousness, there is less dependence on the historical and material components of that religion. Thus, Hegel sees an historical and anthropological shift between the consciousness that relies upon representation and the consciousness that progresses to produce

---

20. Hegel, *Philosophy of Mind*, 302.
21. Hegel, *Encyclopaedia Logic*, 32.

conceptualization. In Hegel's view, the religious consciousness *re-presents* the sensual content, but the representation at the same time provokes the philosophical consciousness to work free of the matter in which that content was initially encountered. "External" features come to be recognized as such. Perhaps now the matter of the "historical Jesus" does not matter and may historically explain the spate of books on that topic launched by Hegelians after Hegel. As that content maintains an element of its temporal or accidental character in the awareness of the subject, philosophical awareness begins to subjugate the sensual form. The content of the religious representation now begins to lift itself above its sensual constraints.

Philosophical Consciousness and True Religion

It is no accident that Hegel scholars for the most part regard Hegel as a monist, for Hegel is intent on reconciling the spirit to Spirit, and part of his philosophical point seems to position the human subject and the Spirit on the same plane and ultimately with the same identity. Calvin believes in the progressive realization of the Christian religion, but is substantially unlike Hegel in the philosopher's monistic leanings. Calvin also believes the movements of human and divine history have been prescribed by God, rather than Hegel's Reason. Calvin and much of the Reformed tradition, however, do seem to place the path of true religion at significant distance from material or sensual things. Hegel and the Reformed thinkers seem to regard closeness to God most coming through the human mind, while Mind is Hegel's philosophical and religious summit.

Emphasis on the commensurability of the human mind with the mind of God has strong emphasis in the pursuit of true religion, as we saw earlier in Zwingli. So too, Calvin writes,

> That in these things consist the true and sincere worship which alone God approves, and in which alone He delights, is both taught by the Holy Spirit throughout the Scriptures, and is also, antecedent to discussion, the obvious dictate of piety. Nor from the beginning was there any other method of worshipp-ing God, the only difference being, that this spiritual truth, which with us is naked and simple, was under the former dispensation wrapt up in figures. And this is the meaning of our Saviour's words, 'The hour cometh, and now is, when the true worshippers shall worship the Father in spirit and in truth' (John IV. 23). For by these words he meant not to declare that God was not worshipped by the fathers

in this spiritual manner, but only to point out a distinction in the external form, viz., That while they had the Spirit shadowed forth by many figures, we have it in simplicity. But it has always been an acknowledged point, that God, who is a Spirit, must be worshipped in spirit and in truth. Moreover, the rule which distinguishes between pure and vitiated worship is of universal application, in order that we may not adopt any device which seems fit to ourselves, but look to the injunctions of Him who alone is entitled to prescribe.[22]

There are significant points to notice here. First, Calvin contends that worshipping God in spirit and in truth has been acknowledged by thoughtful people in all ages, which, therefore, would render it a truth accessible to the non-Christian thinker. Such a truth is not the privileged truth of the Christian thinker. Rather, it is a part of what the theologians call general (universal) or natural revelation. Calvin virtually admits this same point in a passage from the *Institutes*: "In the same way superstition seems to take its name from its not being contented with the measures which reason prescribes, but accumulating a superfluous mass of vanities. But to say nothing more of words, it has been universally admitted in all ages, that religion is vitiated and perverted whenever false opinions are introduced into it . . ."[23]

Calvin's view here derives from his unwillingness to distinguish any particular kind of "Christian" idolatry from any other idolatry: "It is an error to suppose that there is any difference between this madness and that of the heathen."[24] Calvin received fresh impetus to this view from the historical work of Bullinger, the successor of Zwingli, entitled *Decades,* published in 1549. The idolatry of pagans, Israelites, and Christians is significantly on a par because Calvin finds the problem of idolatry arising from human psychology, no matter how the errors of religion are compounded by false teaching and opportunistic priests. Giuseppe Scavizzi, an astute observer of the Reformation attack on images, makes the following remark that would seem to apply also to Calvin:

> It is ironic that Erasmus and Zwingli—who had staged a war on behalf of a renascence of Christian ideals against what they called paganism—defended the pagans against the current interpretation of their religion; but their defence was not accidental, because

22. Calvin, *NRE* 34: 460/Beveridge, *Tracts and Treatises*, Vol. I: 127–28.
23. Calvin, *ICR* 31: 141/Beveridge, *Institutes,* Book I: 104.
24. Calvin, *NRE* 34: 462/Beveridge, *Tracts and Treatises*, Vol. I: 131.

> *their idea of paganism did not indicate a historical era but a way of living and thinking* . . . ancient wisdom came to be regarded more and more in a way not different from that of the humanists. However, as the Reformers agreed, similar wisdom was granted by God to all peoples, Christian and non-Christian . . . Thus in its most elevated form, the religion of the Arabs confirmed the existence of a 'natural' and correct way of understanding the divine even outside revelation. Their manner coincided with that of the enlightened Gentiles and Jews and only the religion of the popes was at variance with it.[25] (Italics mine.)

Whereas Catholics and Luther had generally maintained that the use of images is natural to humankind, Calvin too agreed, but judged the practice as virtually proving a universal inclination to idolatry. One consequence of this estimation is that the cognitive element of religion becomes prominent in personal religion at the expense of other elements, and virtually by default simply because little else is trusted. The question to be asked, however, is whether the intensity of personal experiential religion sought in the notion of true religion can be achieved while supplanting or rejecting the place of sensual components. In this transformation of religious consciousness, the Reformed measures of religious reform generally move toward a philosophical consciousness as depicted by Hegel. We witness in the Reformed tradition and Hegel's philosophy argument for eclipse of the need or at least doubt over the efficacy of the prior sensual and pictorial thinking that had been previously prominent in religious consciousness. In philosophical consciousness, however, this is treated as an intermediate step in intellectual or spiritual ascendancy. In Reformed religion, some allusion to materiality can hardly be avoided, but is in many cases given a "spiritual," that is, a desensualized interpretation. Often spiritual worship is juxtaposed and contrasted to the "splendid glare" of worship incorporating material elements.

In Hegel's thinking, philosophical cognition sidelines the pictorial and imagistic conceptions of art and religion. The use of material things for the understanding of God is in Hegel's estimation devotion in need of closing the distance between itself and the Infinite spirit. This is accomplished by a receding of the sensual in deference to the spiritual. In Hegel's mind, Protestant religion advances over sacramental religion's understanding of the Incarnation because the Catholic worshipper stays bound and stuck to the

---

25. Scavazzi, *Controversy on Images*, 149.

material event, while in philosophical religion, the finite spirit is ushered away from the sensuous to the desensualized Spirit. The intervening sensual mediations are now sidelined for the clear advance of the finite toward the infinite. The Reformed attempt to raise religious understanding by the trimming of material media uncannily begins to resemble the progressive realization of Spirit in Hegel's system.[26]

True Religion and Modern Practice

Among the most noticeable historical changes occurring at the time of the Reformation and extending into the seventeenth century was that of two worlds being rebuilt. The material world was desacralized and the spiritual world dematerialized. But this explanation cannot exempt attention to the relationship of those events to the huge sense of optimism the Protestant Reformation gave to many adherents. For with the Reformation, the experience of lay and ordinary people received huge stimulus in terms of Protestant ideas and doctrines, that, as stated by the Marxist historian Christopher Hill, made men stand up. Part of this standing contributed to the rise of national movements for democracy and to other events, like the Industrial Revolution. In other words, Protestantism put people in motion in a way that had few prior historical parallels. In trying to explain something of how this happened within Protestantism, Hill, in his *Change and Continuity*, writes:

> What mattered was that Protestantism appealed, as medieval heresy had done, to artisans and small merchants, whom it helped to trust the dictates of their own hearts as their standard of conduct. The elect were those who felt themselves to be the elect. What was astonishing was that so many people had at the same time the same miraculous experience of conversion: thanks to God's direct intervention, grace made them free. It could indeed be inexplicable if we could not see that the psychological states leading up to conversion were the effects of a social crisis which hit many unprivileged small producers in the same sort of way. There was no salvation in the old priestly magic, because that no longer gave

---

26. It is notable that Abraham Kuyper, the famous Dutch Calvinist and nineteenth century Prime minister of the Netherlands in his *Lectures on Calvinism*, 149, makes reference to Hegel to argue that "For Calvinism to have had its own art style would have been to slide back to a lower level of religious life. Its nobler effort must be to release religion and divine worship more and more from its sensual form and to encourage its vigorous spirituality."

them any sense of control over the world of economic fluctuations in which they now had to live. Only an assertive self-confidence could do this, and that was so novel that it must seem to come arbitrarily from outside... The social situation set large numbers of men and women seeking answers to similar problems. As, thanks to a Luther, a Calvin, a Zwingli, a group of men realized that 'the object of [Christ's] struggle was to raise up those who were lying prostrate', this in its turn redoubled their confidence.[27]

But if the new confidence bolstered such persons with a willingness to take risks to acquire riches, the same might not be said for the religious piety of the Reformed tradition. For here optimism gave way to the hard realism of a religious life that would be undertaken and lived with few of the former pieces of a sacramental religion linked as it was to the material world. In Reformation devotion, one was not venturesome, but disciplined to a fault. By this I mean that Reformed religious worship and devotion stayed close to Protestant Principle and remained steadfastly suspicious of Catholic Substance. There would be no Baroque additions in this Christian devotion, no unneeded material clutter because such things were specious and quite unnecessary as devotional aids, simply because Christ was sufficient for these austere Protestant peoples. The style of worship would simply be simple—bowings and scrapings and such were distraction and delusion. The new devotee of Protestantism might nevertheless doubt his own derisions of those previous things at times and maybe even ashamedly but privately wish for them on occasions of spiritual drought. However, and as stated by Ozment, the Protestant as a Protestant most of the time preferred a little with some level of certainty, rather than risk a lot on dubious religious objects and practices that veered more toward mechanical routine or seductive splendour, for example, than simply following Christ.

The Protestant optimism that started it all, however, was not quite so much the stuff of secular sociology, as Christopher Hill believes, but something that made this rather strained devotional regimen willingly undertaken. This came from the realization that Christ had brought the sinner to God and that the devotee was needful of Christ alone. The sinner could be and likely was exhausted after his tumultuous journey to Christ, but reaching his destination provided rest at the foot of the Cross, where he could now stand up, unencumbered by past mistakes. He afterward came away exuberant and a new man of the world in Christ because of

---

27. Hill, *Change and Continuity*, 91–92.

it. He was made more alive than ever, for he felt freed from past sorts of religious anxieties, and some anxieties had certainly been cast by the pale of medieval pieties and practices that now must have seemed largely pointless and wasteful and therefore wrong to him. Moreover, because a sinner's salvation previously believed well-nigh impossible was, in Protestant faith, a present reality, there was stupendous relief from the wages of the sins of the self for the sinless living Christ, who set spiritually dead men free to now live physically for him. Perhaps most of all, out of this kind of salvific experience, the followers least wanted to give offense to their Saviour.

This kind of religious release and consequent satisfaction—where before there had been rumblings and tremors and splendid but also cumbersome rituals and pilgrimages—was sociologically the stuff of change and revolution elsewhere. Inside the individual and the Church and the state, it let loose individual and religious and political aspirations, largely unmatched in Western history to that period. But if the epoch-making Protestant optimism generated by overcoming the doom of the sinner damned outside of Christ was good news, it also put in saved Christian hearts an inducement and warning to indeed stay the course and to find all sufficiency in Christ the Sufficient. But for the radical and steadfast distinction within orthodox Protestantism between the saviour Christ and the exceptionless failed humanity, mysticism might have served Protestant devotion more than it did, but mysticism simply smacked too much of a gentlemen's agreement for the stark realism of Protestant anthropology to venture such a path. Nevertheless, one can note much of the aspiration in later Reformed Puritan devotional writing which evidences something like the excruciating mystical search to be taken up into Christ. Some forms of the Puritan experience therefore are not so dissimilar to some of the mystical yearnings of the prior medieval mystics.[28]

Of course, readers may deduce that this book has not been about encouraging the strenuous path of Christian devotion, but making allowances for the weaknesses of human nature. Rather, I have intended to critique the assumption of Christian traditions pulling out all of the props, and particularly material components, for the various reasons discussed in this book,

---

28. For example, in Jonathan Edwards's "Personal Narrative" are these words: "The person of Christ appeared ineffably excellent, with an excellency great enough to swallow up all thought and conception . . . I felt withal, an ardency of soul to be what I know not otherwise how to express, than to be emptied and annihilated; to lie in the dust, and to be full of Christ alone . . ." Quoted in Hatch and Stout, *Jonathan Edwards*, 206.

and then assuming the devotee should live like a saint without them.[29] Moreover, the Protestant experience may easily slip into a spiritual desert brought about in part by devaluing spiritual engagement incorporating material things. The Protestant perhaps takes too much out, whereas the Catholic probably kept too much. Nevertheless, in sectors of Protestantism, the much leaner devotional practice may inadvertently have precipitated not the notion of the sufficiency of Christ, but paradoxically the sufficiency of the devotee. Because Christ is deemed to be sufficient for life, the bridges between Christ and the devotee are pulled up. The resulting kind of devotional life might be compared to walking on water to Christ—until suspicions arise that the water could be construed as a possible mediator pre-empting Christ.

This kind of eradication of suspect elements of devotion may provoke despair. It might also provoke a kind of utopianism, where devotional aids are swept aside as unnecessary and potentially idolatrous, but with a kind of spiritual autonomy being presumed—that perhaps laid some seeds for later modern secular autonomy. The presumption in this path is partly the assumption that the weaknesses and needs of the devotee are met in Christ's sufficiency. Indeed they will be, but this is the culminating victory and finish line of our union with Christ realized. This kind of optimism can mesh into utopianism, and thus easily slide into a kind of spiritual self-sufficiency or pride.

Nevertheless, the traditional argument for caution in the use of material components can be seen in another example from Calvin's *On the Necessity of Reforming the Church*, where he complains,

> For while it is incumbent on true worshippers to give the heart and the mind, men are always desirous to invent a mode of serving God of a totally different description, their object being to perform to him certain bodily observances, and keep the mind to themselves. Moreover they imagine that when they obtrude upon him external pomp, they have, by this artifice, evaded the necessity of giving themselves. And this is the reason why they submit to innumerable observances which miserably fatigue them

---

29. Indeed, this assumption manifests itself in the change of definition of who the saint is between Catholicism and Protestantism. In contrast to Catholicism's exalted and venerated list of saints, Protestantism has insisted, following in large part the habit of St. Paul in his letters of the New Testament, to designate Christians qua Christians, as "saints." This change certainly, and rightly I think, accommodates the Protestant theological understanding of salvation, and also rightly underlines the extraordinary egalitarian mercy of the Christian God extended to an undeserving humanity.

without measure and without end, and why they chose to wander in a perpetual labyrinth, rather than worship God simply in spirit and truth . . . For were the option given, there is nothing which the carnal man would not prefer to do rather than consent to worship God as prescribed by our doctrine. It is easy to use the words faith and repentance, but the things are most difficult to perform. He, therefore, who makes the worship of God consist in these, by no means loosens the reins of discipline, but compels men to the course which they are most afraid to take. Of this we have most pregnant proof from fact. Men will allow themselves to be restricted by numerous severe laws, to be obliged to numerous laborious observances, to wear a severe and heavy yoke; in short, there is no annoyance to which they will not submit, provided there is no mention of the heart. Hence, it appears that there is nothing to which the human mind is more averse than to that spiritual truth which is the constant topic of our sermons, and nothing with which it is more engrossed than that splendid glare on which our adversaries so strongly insist.[30]

The problem issues in the human resistance encountered in giving heart and mind—indeed all—to God. That is, there is the encouragement of religious devotion uncoupled from traditional material elements, such as "certain bodily observances" precipitously used to expedite devotion all too eager to escape true devotion to God. In the passage, we see the personal experiential emphasis distance itself from material media by way of contrast drawn between internal and external devotion. The prominence of personal religion, therefore, is achieved without many of the traditional aids to devotion because in Calvin's view, they do not function as aids, but instead as impediments to devotion. They are objects and exercises that present a pretense of atoning objectivity. The aids are largely undermined by Calvin as being unbeneficial liabilities for real religion.

Calvin, as a second generation Protestant Reformer, believed that the Protestant Reformation was unfinished, despite his great respect for Luther. He writes, "When Luther at first appeared, he merely touched, with a gentle hand, a few abuses of the grossest description, now grown intolerable." But in the next sentence, Calvin portends in mild manner the disagreements that eventually surface with Lutherans over proper worship by asserting that "And he did it with a modesty which intimated that he had more desire to see them corrected, than determination to correct them himself."[31] For

---

30. Calvin, *NRE* 34: 479/Beveridge, *Tracts and Treatises*, Vol. I: 153–54.
31. Calvin, *NRE* 34: 499/Beveridge, *Tracts and Treatises*, Vol. I: 183.

Denuded Devotion to Christ

Calvin, the principal way in which the work of the Reformation remained after Luther was in the matter of religious worship, and when pressed by Catholic opponents on the accomplishment of his measures of reform, Calvin immediately goes to the correction of idolatry and its familiar associations: "But the pretence that no benefit has resulted from our doctrine is most false. I say nothing of the correction of external idolatry, and of numerous superstitions and errors; though that is not to be counted of no moment. But is there no fruit in this, that many who are truly pious feel their obligation to us, in that they have at length learned to worship God with a pure heart..."[32]

For Calvin, true religion is virtually synonymous with true devotion. In *The Necessity of Reforming the Church*, he goes so far as to say, "If it be inquired, then, by what things chiefly the Christian religion has a standing existence amongst us, and maintains its truth, it will be found that the following two not only occupy the principal place, but comprehend under them all the other parts, and consequently the whole substance of Christianity, viz., a knowledge, first, of the mode in which God is duly worshipped; and secondly, of the source from which salvation is to be obtained. When these are kept out of view, though we may glory in the name of Christians, our profession is empty and vain."[33]

The significance of this passage is that in it Calvin seems to place correct worship on a par with the central and guiding principle of the Protestant Reformation: *sola fide*. In his "Reply by John Calvin to Cardinal Sadolet's Letter," he remarks, "You afterwards come nearer to the point, when you show that there is nothing more pestiferous to souls than a perverse worship of God..."[34]

When Calvin comes to consider what is meant by the due worship of God, he writes, "To this is united adoration, by which we manifest for Him the reverence due to his greatness and excellency, and to this ceremonies are subservient, as helps or instruments, in order that, in the performance of divine worship, the body may be exercised at the same time with the soul."[35]

However, though "ceremonies" here are given a guarded legitimacy by Calvin, there follows in none of the remaining treatise any positive

---

32. Calvin, *NRE* 34: 511/Beveridge, *Tracts and Treatises*, Vol. I: 200.
33. Calvin, *NRE* 34: 459/Beveridge, *Tracts and Treatises*, Vol. I: 126.
34. Calvin, *RS* 33: 388/Beveridge, *Tracts and Treatises*, Vol. I: 29.
35. Calvin, *NRE* 34: 460/Beveridge, *Tracts and Treatises*, Vol. I: 127.

elaboration of their role in religious worship. Sprinkled throughout the treatise, moreover, are continued warnings against the abuse of ceremony. He makes a differentiation among religious worshippers similar to that in the prior passage from Zwingli by saying that "Of ceremonies, indeed, you have more than enough, but, for the most part, so childish in their import, and vitiated by innumerable forms of superstition, as to be utterly unavailing for the preservation of the Church . . . Ceremonies we have in a great measure abolished, but we were compelled to do so, partly because by their multitude they had degenerated into a kind of Judaism, partly because they filled the minds of the people with superstition, and could not possibly remain without doing the greatest injury to the piety which it was their office to promote."[36]

The Philosophical Consciousness and Protestant Possibilities

The Reformed tradition, much like many other Protestant traditions at the time of the Reformation, in desiring to go past the Christian medieval scholastic traditions with their "arid" rationalism, found a natural alliance with the much earlier Christian tradition of the Church Fathers, and of course earlier still, with the Bible. To the majority of the Protestant Reformers, this earlier tradition of the Fathers manifested a Christian spiritual life and vitality that for various historical reasons had significantly declined during the later medieval scholastic era. When in particular the works of Aristotle came into familiarity and then vogue among the scholastics of the thirteenth century, the potency of his philosophy as an articulated reasoned account of man and the world raised the stakes for a Christian synthesis that needed due caution over reason having the last word in placing philosophical judgment over and against Christian revelation.

The classical notion of a "Christian philosophy" prominent among Christian thinkers like Justin Martyr and Clement of Alexandria was resurrected over a millennium later among Reformers such as Erasmus and Calvin, as we saw in chapter 3. However, the Christian philosophy of these thinkers would go to the Bible and the Church Fathers for their Christian philosophy, in contrast to the notorious medieval scholastic tradition that had preceded them. Moreover, some of the new and emerging monastic traditions in the early second millennium had likewise emphasized the

---

36. Calvin, *RS* 33: 395/Beveridge, *Tracts and Treatises*, Vol. I: 39.

earlier tradition of the Church Fathers, rather than simply trying to scholastically couple reason and religious belief.

A figure representative of this Catholic monastic movement and an extraordinary personage of that era was Bernard of Clairvaux, 1090–1153. Bernard was very critical of the philosophers of his day, as were the later Protestant Reformers, and his battle with the Scholastic Peter Abelard is famous. Moreover, while it has been commonplace for historians to see antecedents of Protestantism in ventures such as the Brethren of the Common Life and works like *The Imitation of Christ*, antecedents also came from some of this prior monastic tradition, such as that represented by Bernard and his Cistercian order. This is especially to be noted since Bernard is also renowned for his rather severe notions about a genuine Christian piety or devotion, coupled with his warnings that the aesthetic lure of devotion could prove dangerous to that devotion.

Protestantism drew some impetus—though Protestants would object to monasticism as an institution—from a monastic reform movement of this kind. The reason was simple. Some energetic monastic reformers like Bernard pulled away from the pleasures of sense so loved by other and more luxuriant pieties of the Middle Ages because in his view, that fed into spiritual laxity. Many later Protestant communities also expressed reservation and sometimes revulsion at many of these materialistic pieties, to include the kind on display in quarters of the opulent Rome. The opposition of the Cistercians, moreover, toward the senses and the liabilities of the senses is seen in the Cistercian aesthetic of the plain style and prefigures much of the later Protestantism, though without the walls of the cloister.

This trimmed and diminutive aesthetic is reflected in Cistercian life and literature and reflects a perspective where religious venerations are esteemed metaphysically and materially slighted. In such a reform of religious devotion that could conceivably be characterized also as movement from sense to transcendence, this skeletal aesthetic moves toward a metaphysical edifice while spurning the unreformed appetites of sense as spiritually detrimental and dangerous. Simplicity, as in the Protestant Reformed tradition, arises as the prevailing aesthetic and the one conducive to rigorous Christian devotion.

The disciplining of the senses for purposes of the spiritual within the Cistercians may be also interpreted as another historical example of attempting to negate the spurious need of the human religious consciousness for material associations, the same point we considered with the Protestant

Reformed tradition of the sixteenth century and also see in Hegel in the nineteenth century. This reforming edifice of the twelfth century among the Cistercians, moreover, purports to rise above a popular piety mired in the earthy tangles of much material religious piety. Thus, the Cistercian Bernard attempts a religious life averse to popular sensual religious appetites. The provocation for the triumph of spiritual thought over textures in this aesthetic seems poised with the belief that a desensualized religious piety not only trumps other means of spiritual approximation, but renders them unnecessary and superfluous. While he was willing to admit that lay populations would need the embrace of the sensual for matters of the spirit, he believed that for the cloistered monks, sensual imagery should be avoided.

As efforts for religious reform continued within medieval Christendom, and particularly so among the emerging monastic orders of the thirteenth century, some of the most notable Christians of this period urged the prescription that Christ-followers should abandon superfluity and excess, which hindered rather than helped those set for spiritual seriousness in their walk to Christ. A singular focus on Christ expedited such a walk. To walk the Christian walk, one must walk with him and with nothing but him.

The items evaluated as impediments to such a journey were varied, but a particular phrase and idea that caught fire and can perhaps first be attributed to St. Jerome of the fifth century was "naked to follow naked the naked Christ." The idea was to impugn lavishness while implying material poverty for a life lived with few to no possessions, for unprofitable competition and compromise ensue when we have or use anything besides Christ to abide with Christ. Such was, for example, the tendency of Francis of Assisi and Clare and many around them, to virtually transpose the meaning of "naked to follow the naked Christ" to mean poor to follow the poor Christ. And, as one of those later significant preludes to Protestantism, the fifteenth century work, the *Imitation of Christ*, admonishes its readers to "Strive for this, pray for this, desire this, to be stripped of all selfishness and naked follow the naked Jesus, to die to self and live forever for me."[37]

However, as a stringent critic of the Cluny monastic movement, St. Bernard represents something more akin to the mindset of the later

---

37. Kempis, *Imitation*, 86. R. W. Southern writes that in the prior Catholic notion, "The 'whole Gospel' meant following Christ in poverty and stark simplicity of life: *paupers pauperem Christum seequentes*. This was not yet quite the 'imitation of Christ' as it later came to be conceived, but it was a step in this direction." Southern, *Western Society*, 252.

Denuded Devotion to Christ

Protestant Reformed tradition that also willed a further reformation of the Protestant Lutheran tradition. The Cistercian order that Bernard belonged to was as ardent as any other order for encouraging austere spiritual effort to affect closeness to Christ. However, Bernard did not precisely see wealth as the enemy of the soul. In other words, it was not literally acquisitiveness and property that were the problem, but rather the potentially dangerous delights that the Creator provided the human with in His world. It was not precisely buildings, for example, (as in St. Francis) that one was to shrink from, but beautiful buildings that one should avoid.[38]

What precisely was Bernard pursing in trimming down the devotional life to the things that really mattered, coupled with his aversion to the dry rationalism of the scholastic tradition of his day? A suggestive answer has been offered by Josef Pieper.

> Plainly, Bernard's passionate and truly "philosophical" interest was directed toward full "realization," toward existential Wholeness, which is to say "salvation." And he regarded all forms of human expression, his philosophizing as well as his theology, as designed to serve that Whole. It was precisely this kind of salvation that Bernard considered to be endangered and undermined by "dialecticians" of the type of Abelard. The danger which he quite rightly saw dawning in such personalities, and which he fought with all his might, was nothing less than this: that the substance of Truth, by which living man is nourished, would be consumed by an empty formalism of "correct" thinking—consumed and reduced to the vanishing point. "Burning," said Bernard, had to be added to knowledge. By the end of his life, when he had all but burned

---

38. Interestingly enough, the aversion to the material world religiously, in this tradition, gave the material world secular prominence, as we see in the label of "puritan" applied to the Cistercians. Thus Southern writes of this Catholic order that "These puritans of the monastic life incurred the penalty of puritanism; they became rich because they renounced the glory of riches, and powerful because they invested wisely. They were blamed for being rich and powerful by those who went out for glory and invested badly or not at all." *Western Society*, 260–61. With more specific regard to the religious suspicion of material accompaniments in religious practice, we might consider Bernard's criticism of his contemporary, Abbot Suger, for the latter's perceived excesses: "Oh vanity! Vanity! and folly even greater than vanity! The church sparkles and gleams on all sides, while its poor huddle in need; its stones are gilded, while its children go unclad; in it the art lovers find enough to satisfy their curiosity, while the poor find nothing to relieve their misery." Quoted in Scott, *The Gothic Enterprise*, 155–56. Fueling this kind of derision, moreover, was Bernard's fear that the opulence of the cloister of his monks might impede their devotion to God because of their attraction to the beauty of the architecture. Here we witness the fear and hesitation toward beauty spoken of by Mary Warnock in chapter 4.

True Religion and the Philosophical Consciousness

> himself away, he summed up this philosophy in a succinct and memorable phrase ... The whole thing is said in only three words: *anima quaerens Verbum* ... "The soul in search of the Word." But, he explains, the Word can be found only by the going out of oneself (ecstasies) of mystic contemplation in which the soul "enjoys the Word." What in truth happens in that state cannot be communicated in human language: *ineffable est*. This, we may say, was the essential message of the mystic Bernard of Clairvaux.[39]

Pieper notes that prominent among the scholastics was a notion of truth, small t, that would be insufficient to live the Christian life, according to Bernard, for in the end what sufficed for the scholastics was an empty formalism of correct thinking, or what we might call dead orthodoxy, and what Bernard might say would be sufficiently deadly to kill a living faith. In other words, Christian faith had to be kept alive because the Word it served was alive. This concentrated desire might push religious devotion toward mysticism of a sort, as it did in Bernard, but for Protestants this same desire would be without the trek toward a mysticism of the kind poised toward communion with the ineffable wordless Word. Any notion that words are not sufficient for an understanding of the divine as found in Christian mystical traditions finds little resonance in later Protestant religion.[40]

Nevertheless, Bernard shares in the predilection of some sectors of Protestantism to exhibit aversion toward the things of sense in the proper worship of God. The Cistercians of course are notable for their plain style and the attempt, it seems, largely by Bernard, to erase the physical and sensual components of life from the mind in communion with God. However, for all of the powerful influence of Bernard upon his order, this would prove to be an ideal that would falter. Historian Christopher Brooke cites a material example of what happened in the very year of Bernard's death within his own order. Perhaps the event of the change reveals the stresses of a spirituality lived without the accompaniment of the senses.

> Even Bernard's own Clairvaux acquired an apse when he was securely dead. To a man like Bernard a large apse could represent

---

39. Pieper, *Scholasticism*, 90.

40. Alston, "Religion," 143: "Prophetic religion, unlike the others, stresses the *word* as the medium of contact with the divine. (An example is the opening of the Gospel of John.) For the ritualist, and still more for the mystic, whatever words he may use, the consummation of his endeavors is found in a wordless communion with the divine. *In prophetic religion, however, the linguistic barrier is never let down; it is not felt as a barrier at all*." (Italics mine.)

the essence of contemporary traditional Benedictine fashion: a semicircle of alluring light and color—or dark mysterious painting—that provided a frame for a glistening altar and perhaps a glorious shrine, the essence of distraction. In a Cistercian church a plain wooden altar sat in front of a plain stone wall, with windows round to let in the light so that the priest and the sacrament could be seen. No doubt variety would have come in any case; what is surprising is that so great a degree of uniformity seems to have been preserved so long. No doubt one must not insist too precisely on the coincidence of dates. Yet when all is said and done the outbreak of apses is eloquent testimony to the urges Bernard had held in check.[41]

So matter is left out with matters of the spirit for Bernard, much like the Protestant thinkers I have considered in this work. For this reason, and as I indicated in the preface, this spiritualizing point of view is by no means solely confined to the thinkers I have addressed, but can be rather easily found in other Christian traditions. That being said, I would nevertheless contend that it is largely foreign to a Christian religion that affirms the goodness of the material world and a goodness confirmed in the most substantial way in the event of God coming to material humans in material human form in Jesus the Christ. To set aside the senses and the material world in the worship of the Christian God is virtually akin to the nearly universal propensity among many other world religions to relegate matter to the periphery in consideration of matters of the spirit.[42]

However, in the sector of Protestantism that I have surveyed, the worshipper may give allegiance to the Word largely only in the presence of words, reflecting a suspicion of the resonances of matter with a proper spiritual life. This devotion, however, commits this kind of religious understanding and devotion to work much like a philosopher. Moreover, the hesitation cast on matter, images, the senses, and beauty—among the varieties

---

41. Brooke, *Age of the Cloister*, 180–81.

42. Interestingly, the noted Hindu thinker of the twentieth century, Sri Aurobindo Ghose, made the following observation in *The Supramental Manifestation*, 7, "In the past the body has been regarded by spiritual seekers rather as an obstacle, as something to be overcome and discarded, than as an instrument of spiritual perfection and a field of the spiritual change." This of course is from a Hindu thinker, whose religious tradition has been rather notorious for slighting the material world and the body for spiritual purposes. That a religious tradition like that of Christianity with its affirmation of the material world would subscribe to something similar to what Aurobindo describes is surely a matter of perplexity.

of the sensible—seems assured in truncating matter for the communion of spirits. Thus, Lady Philosophy's rebuke of her languishing prisoner Boethius can be extended into an exhortation to make even the "ordinary dull-witted man" into a philosopher. By minding his philosophical manners, he should see, for example, that truth for the sake of the truth should be sufficient to claim his allegiance even in jail and the throes of death, just as it might in a denuded Christian worship in a church scraped from top to bottom of distracting matter, for purposes of spiritual concentration.

However, though neither mystics nor monists, Protestants can nevertheless accommodate some of Bernard's spiritual goal, as it is set on Christ, indeed, as oneness with Christ, as Pieper indicates. However, even in Bernard's case, we find the shunning of the senses and matter. The besetting problem in Protestantism has been the desire for a spiritual communion much like that of Bernard, but unlike Bernard, not for an ineffable wordless Word. In the desire for the Protestant communion with God, there is of course not an empty truth pursued, but something like a naked devotion or spirituality. What was that like? R. W. Southern writes of the Brethren of the Common Life that, "In contrast to those for whom the faith was simply a matter of formal adherence or intellectual assent, Groote's followers sought an effective, personal, experimental faith. Their detestation of merely formal religion was unbounded. What they wished to put in its place was something that they could never define, but it is abundantly illustrated in their spiritual diaries and collections of *memorabilia*."[43]

We see here allusion to the suspicion of form and structure as dulling if not suffocating authentic religious life. Therefore, one can circumvent and substitute the fervent for the formal and so too spiritual autobiography for art in some way, as the default art. And yet, the noticeable point with reference to this kind of spirituality is the description of it as one "they could never define." The question to ask, moreover, is, Why not?

This is the question of this book, and my suggestion of an answer is that no answer was forthcoming because this endeavor has largely been tried without benefit of matter for spiritual advance, paralleled in part by revulsion toward form as the enemy of authenticity. One might say, then, that as a result, they were largely on their own with God. This could again have made of them mystics, when instead it made a significant and historically important portion of them, Puritans. It does appear at times as if their religion is something of a do-it-yourself-religion, but this is, I think, from

---

43. Southern, *Western Society*, 354.

fear of being an inauthentic Christian; thus, they were very careful. They tried to advance the spiritual life with spirit—as the heavenly angels—and not as restored earthlings, while they nevertheless in great part remade the earth and built with manifest influence, the modern world.

On the other hand, it was better historically perhaps to have both traditions—each reminding the other of something needful and something each might forget were it not for the other. One went too far with too much, but the other went with too little. It has been with one Protestant tradition within the latter that I have tried to indicate some insufficient but still understandable reasons why.

Afterword

True Religion and Puritan Consciousness

(INASMUCH AS THIS BOOK WAS SIGNIFICANTLY PROVOKED BY MY EXPERIence within Protestant Evangelical culture years ago, I have appended in this afterword some thoughts on the contemporary Evangelical situation, such as are not perhaps dissimilar with some of the issues written about in the chapters of this book.)

In *The Scandal of the Evangelical Mind*, Mark Noll has perhaps written the most poignant volume to date on the unease of Evangelical believers with using the intellect.[1] In this work, Noll catalogues the devastating costs for denying religious attention to matters of the mind, while he engages particular historical episodes to explain the rift of the intellect and the Evangelical. However, a huge component of the Evangelical scandal is missed if that scandal is only seen as the separation of the Evangelical believer from the intellect.

In the Evangelical scandal at large, it is understandably omission of the mind from Evangelical religious life and practice that draws the most attention and therefore the most lamenting. For those who see in the urgency of a practical commitment to the saving of souls no time and ultimately no value in saving the mind, matters of the intellect cannot matter because they do not engage the central or perhaps exclusive matter in such a conception: the heart or the soul. Attention to this aspect of the Evangelical scandal alone, however, can mask the fact that a different kind of problem may exist even among those Evangelical believers who embrace the intellect.

While there is certainly much resistance by many Evangelical believers toward seriously enlisting the intellect in the cause of the Gospel, that resistance must be coupled with the fact that when Evangelical embrace of the intellect occurs, it very often excludes other significant components of the

1. Noll, *Scandal*.

human person and human experience. Thus, while there are two factions in the war over the mind versus no mind in Evangelicalism, being on the side of mind does not close the door to all that Noll refers to as the scandal of the Evangelical mind. This fact alone indicates that the Evangelical Scandal is not solely about the separation of the Evangelical from the intellect. For while Noll argues for the integration of the Christian faith with all learning, he complains against those Evangelicals who do give credence to the importance of intellect, that their focus is too narrowly *theological*. Moreover, Noll asks how an Evangelical tradition steeped in and devoted to the biblical belief that God is the author and sustainer of nature, various human and good institutions, and beauty, evidences little comparative attention to the study of such subjects. That is, Evangelical *theological* thought, which Noll concedes as robust and rigorous, manifests the fact that in the Evangelical scandal, "The problem concerns rather the connections between theology and other forms of learning."[2]

Negligent in attention to the wider intellectual bridges needed to span from biblical truth to all truth, American Evangelicalism, despite its theological acumen, has jeopardized the construction of a robust Evangelical mind by creating a mind too narrowly focused on theology. Thus, for Noll, any scandal of the Evangelical mind does not disappear—though of course it will shrink—when the intellect is permitted to work. The Evangelical scandal therefore is not a problem resolved simply or only by embracing the intellect.

Noll comes close to articulating why Evangelicals are not diligent with subjects outside theology when he makes the telling observation that the disparagement of the mind in Evangelicalism can be deceptive because Evangelicals actually "have much more confidence in their minds than in the evidence of their senses."[3] This point underlies much of Noll's analysis, but he does not appropriate it fully in coming to terms with the larger Evangelical scandal.[4] In this brief essay, moreover, I will attempt to see the Evangelical scandal in terms of lack of engagement with the senses because I will contend that displacing of the senses by the Evangelical mind is a crucial aspect of the scandal of the Evangelical mind. If the missing links between

2. Ibid., 19.
3. Ibid.,175.
4. In conversation with Professor Noll at a conference at Wheaton College around 1997, he indicated to me that he desired very much to develop this point in his book, but that publishing deadlines kept him for such an addition.

theology and other areas of life and culture is a consequence of the selective Evangelical mind, then responsibility for omissions may lie with excessive cautiousness by the Evangelical mind toward the senses. Moreover, this caution may arise from an Evangelical suspicion of the *religious* value of the sensual, material, or physical worlds as opposed to the spiritual. Part of the Evangelical suspicion of the senses is evident not only in what subject matter Evangelicals who do embrace the mind exclude, as Noll suggests, but what parts of themselves they exclude from religious life and attention.

Noll is right to see an aspect of the Evangelical scandal in a robust theological effort that is ironically too narrow. This aspect of the scandal, moreover, needs to be explained as belonging to an Evangelical mind already in place. The primary problem of Evangelicals up to their boots in theology, but little else, is not anti-intellectualism. It may, however, be anti-sensualism.

Focusing on an Evangelical scandal as a scandal concerning the sensual, one must take great care not to misinterpret what took place between the intellectual Puritans and the emotional Evangelical revivals of the nineteenth century—the usual stretch of history to point to while surveying the origin of the Evangelical scandal. Noll rightly presents the Puritans as the "immediate ancestors of American Evangelicals"[5] and he locates the beginning of the end of the Evangelical mind between the American Puritans and the Evangelical revivals. He goes on to locate in the transitional period between the Puritans and revivalism the case of Jonathan Edwards, "the greatest Evangelical mind in American history," and bemoans the fact that among Evangelicals, "Edwards had no intellectual successors."[6] However, in coupling the facts of Edwards—and the Revivals—not following Puritanism, with Evangelicals not following Edwards, but the revivals, we can forget whom those Evangelicals who have not forsaken the theological mind may be following. We may mistakenly take them all to have followed the revivalists. Furthermore, in thinking the revivalists diffused a strong Puritan heritage that should be regained by Evangelicals of today, we may romanticize the Puritans.

Noll's Puritans seem to serve for him as they do for David Wells in the latter's *No Place for Truth*, as a prescriptive model for Evangelicals because they did engage their Christianity with their mind. However, if utilization of the mind does not close the door to all that makes for the Evangelical

5. Ibid., 40.
6. Ibid., 24.

Scandal, then such a recommendation is beside the point. However, we cannot bypass the Puritans this quickly, for there is something else to plumb in considering the Puritans as a model for emulation by Evangelicals. That is, one must address the well-known contention of a spate of historians, of the likes of Max Weber and Perry Miller, for example, that the Puritan mind was cultivated at the expense of the senses and the affections. This charge against the Puritans is scarcely addressed within the Evangelical discussion of the Evangelical Scandal. However, if it is the case that a rift of the intellect from the senses was characteristic of the Puritans, then to beckon for a return to Puritanism as a way of unifying the Evangelical mind is a mistake, if an aspect of the Evangelical scandal is neglect of the senses. A return to Puritanism may recapture the Puritan mind, but that mind may be faulty.

If a rift of the intellect from the senses was characteristic of the Puritans, then it was possibly the vacuum created by such a separation that beckoned the previously denied emotionalism that the Evangelical revivals provided. On this view, the Puritan intellect suffocated the affections until the revivals unleashed them. The Puritans therefore may have inadvertently created the emotional mire in which many of the Evangelical camp, wanting to forego mind, find themselves. The significant point here, moreover, is that though it is usual to fault Evangelicals for not following Puritanism close enough, that aspect of the problem of the scandal concerning the senses may have arisen precisely because Evangelicals followed the Puritans too closely.

If Jonathan Edwards had no Evangelical heirs because his potential followers became emotional and anti-intellectual revivalists, then we may have fixed upon the origin of the scandal of the Evangelical mind, but we cannot fix a contemporary Evangelical reticence with the use of the senses in a revivalist ancestry that embraced them to the detriment of intellect. As noted by George Marsden in his classic *Fundamentalism and American Culture*, "After Edwards' time revivalist theology in America moved steadily toward emphasizing the human side of religious experience."[7] That is, embracing the intellect and shunning the senses is not the legacy of a revivalist mentality. Puritanism then may be the residual source of the Evangelical suspicion of the sensual, and this I contend may be responsible for the narrow theological focus alleged by Noll. Ironically, however, a return to Puritanism is often heralded by Evangelicals as a solution to the problem of the scandal, whereas my contention is that the Puritan influence may be

---

7. Marsden, *Fundamentalism*, 99.

part of the problem. Aware of its own inheritance in Puritanism, Evangelicals seem generally reticent to criticize the mores of a movement to which they owe so much, but which at the same time appears to have excluded too much.

As a residual source of the Evangelical suspicion of the sensual, Puritanism then may be responsible for the list of neglected topics by Evangelicals listed by Noll. A similar point about "neglected topics" was made by historian Richard Lovelace in his *Dynamics of Spiritual Life* and warrants a lengthy quotation from that work:

> In the early years of my Christian life, as a converted intellectual drawing my spiritual nurture from the Evangelical world, I used to wonder why there were no Evangelical poets and novelists of major stature . . . I was convinced that Evangelical Protestantism had a strong hold on biblical truth and spiritual reality, and I was willing to tolerate the fact that it was an aesthetic desert because I was so thirsty for the experience of grace and wisdom which made it an oasis in the desert of the world . . . Gradually through the study of history I was able to track down some of the causes for these problems. I found that Evangelicalism had its roots in Puritan and Pietistic traditions which had fused the ascetic piety of the early church fathers with Protestant doctrine and which had also over-reacted against the luxurious expression of Christian faith in symbolic liturgy, graphic art, music and architecture. As a result of these forces, the Evangelical stream moved away from the sacramental vision of life in Catholic tradition, in which the created world is not only celebrated as good but recognized as a constant symbolic message about spiritual reality. Evangelicals moved almost in a Manichaean direction, toward a frame of mind in which the objects of sense and sight could drag us away from what was spiritual.[8]

Coupling this observation with the statement by Marsden, one arrives at an Evangelical emphasis on the human side of religious experience that resists objects of sense and sight that detract from spirituality. In effect, the human emphasis must leave out some of the human. In his book, Noll refers to the "Intellectual Heresy" that he thinks Evangelicals are most susceptible and reveals, I think, his implicit agreement with the point made by Lovelace. That is, Noll sees the central error the Evangelical perpetually courts as suspicion of the value of the material versus the spiritual. In this

---

8. Lovelace, *Dynamics*, 344–45.

Denuded Devotion to Christ

vein he sees Manichaeism, Gnosticism, and Docetism—I would add strains of Puritan rationalism—as potential bedfellows to guard against. This conviction is most evident at the end of Noll's book where he hands a palm to Evangelicals but also throws down the gauntlet: "The great truth of the Incarnation is that the Son of God became flesh and dwelt among us. In this foundational truth we may emphasize the nature of the Son of Man himself, or we may emphasize his taking on flesh and dwelling among us. The condemning scandal for Evangelicals is that they have neglected this second emphasis and all that it implies about the possibility of thinking about this realm of flesh. Their redeeming scandal is that they have not yet forgotten the first."[9] But while Noll draws attention to the Evangelical reticence over the physical in its preference for the spiritual, he seems to invoke no antecedents in Puritan spiritualized rationalism. But clearly there are Puritan characteristics portending the latter shortcomings of Evangelicals that Noll chronicles. Two of these, the unceremonious aesthetic desert of the "naked Christ," so prized in Puritan theology and worship, and the scorn for any religious practice whose utility is not immediately apparent reverberate throughout Noll's work as criticisms of Evangelicals. Furthermore, Noll seems to see the engine of rationalism in Evangelicalism driven almost entirely by echoes of the Enlightenment, and not by Puritan rationalism. But in noting the absent intellectual thrust of Evangelicalism—outside of theology proper—the reticence of the Evangelical intellect heavily invested in theology to invest "in thinking about this realm of the flesh" may be traceable to reticence over the value and use of the realm of the material for purposes of religious practice and understanding.

Thus, and reminiscent of Noll's lament, perhaps Edwards had no Evangelical heirs because his mode of religious devotion moves into a realm of sensibility rejected by the Puritan inheritance in the Evangelical tradition that continues in the rationalistic intellectualistic mode of Puritan anthropology.

Alistar McGrath, a historian of the Reformation and an Evangelical, has contended that Evangelicals have "neglected to give weight to the human weaknesses and needs that make certain forms of spirituality so attractive an option for many people." After noting that "Evangelicalism is seen to lack a spirituality to give its theology staying power in the modern period," McGrath notes the paradox that the "distinctive feature" of Evangelicalism is a "devotional ethos," but that the Evangelical movement

---

9. Noll, *Scandal*, 252.

has many specialist journals devoted to Evangelical theology, but none to Evangelical Spirituality.[10]

The question waiting for an answer is simply, Why not? It is certainly odd that Evangelicalism has as a defining feature of itself this devotional ethos, and yet scarcely engages that subject in its literature. I fear the answer may have to come forth from Evangelicalism's hesitation toward the realm of the material, as opposed to the realm of the spiritual. One must not forget that God made both and in Christ is redeeming both.

---

10. McGrath, *Evangelicalism*, 124, 130.

Bibliography

Alexander, Bobby. "An Afterward on Ritual in Biblical Studies." *Semeia* 67 (1994) 209-25.
Alston, William. "Religion." In *The Encyclopaedia of Philosophy*. Edited by Paul Edwards. New York: Macmillan, 1967.
Apostolos-Cappadona, Diane. *Art, Creativity and the Sacred: An Anthology in Religion and Art*. New York: Crossroad, 1984.
Aston, Margaret. *England's Iconoclasts*. Oxford: Clarendon, 1988.
———. *Lollards and Reformers: Images and Literacy in Late Medieval Religion*. London: Hambledon, 1984.
Auski, Peter. *Christian Plain Style: The Evolution of a Spiritual Ideal*. Montreal: McGill-Queen's University Press, 1995.
———. "Simplicity and Silence: the Influence of Scripture on the Aesthetic Thought of the Major Reformers." *Journal of Religious History* 10 (1979) 110-23.
Bainton, Roland H. *Erasmus of Christendom*. New York: Scribner, 1969.
———. *Here I Stand: A Life of Martin Luther*. Nashville: Abingdon, 1950.
Baxter, Richard. *The Saints Everlasting Rest*. 9th ed. London: Fracis Tyton and Jane Underhill, 1662.
Bellarmine, Robert. *Disputationes de Controversiis Christianae Fidei*. 1599.
Boethius. *The Consolation of Philosophy*. Mineola, NY: Dover, 2002.
Bouwsma, William J. *John Calvin: A Sixteenth-Century Portrait*. New York: Oxford University Press, 1988.
Bouyer, Louis. *A History of Christian Spirituality*. London: Burns & Oates, 1969.
Brooke, Christopher. *The Age of the Cloister: The Story of Monastic Life in the Middle Ages*. Mahwah, NJ: Hidden Spring, 2003.
Brown, Peter. *Augustine of Hippo: A Biography*. Berkeley: University of California Press, 1967.
Bryer, Anthony, and Judith Herrin, editors. *Iconoclasm*. Birmingham: St. Martin's, 1990.
Brown, Frank Burch. *Religious Aesthetics: A Theological Study of Making and Meaning*. Princeton: Princeton University Press, 1989.
Brown, Normon O. *Life Against Death: The Psychoanalytic Meaning of History*. Middletown, CT: Wesleyan University Press, 1959.
Bullinger, Heinrich. *The Decades*, translated by Thomas Harding. Cambridge: Cambridge University Press, 1852.
Christensen, Carl. *Art and the Reformation in Germany*. Athens: Ohio University Press, 1979.
Daly, Robert. *God's Altar: The World and the Flesh in Puritan Poetry*. Berkeley: University of California Press, 1978.
Davidson, Clifford, and Ann Eljenholm Nichols, editors. *Iconoclasm vs. Art and Drama*. Kalamazoo, MI: Medieval Institute Publications, 1989.

Bibliography

Davies, Horton. *The Worship of the American Puritans*. New Haven: Yale University Press, 1990.
Dawson, Christopher. *The Dividing of Christendom*. New York: Sheed & Ward, 1965.
———. *Religion and the Rise of Western Culture*. Garden City, NY: Doubleday, 1958.
Dickens, A. G. *The English Reformation*. New York: Schocken, 1964.
Dillenberger, John. "The Diversity of Disciplines as a Theological Question: The Visual Arts as Para-digm." *Journal of the American Academy of Religion* 48 (1980) 231–45.
———. *A Theology of Artistic Sensibilities: The Visual Arts and the Church*. New York: Crossroad, 1986.
Dixon, John. *Nature and Grace in Art*. Chapel Hill: University of North Carolina Press, 1964.
———. "When Is Art Religion and When Is Religion Art?" *Semeia* 10 (1988) 123–41.
Eck, Johannes. *On Not Removing Images of Christ and the Saints*, 1523.
Eire, Carlos M. N. *War against the Idols: The Reformation of Worship from Erasmus to Calvin*. New York: Cambridge University Press, 1986.
Eco, Umberto. *The Aesthetics of Thomas Aquinas*. Translated by Hugh Bredin. Cambridge: Harvard University Press, 1988.
———. *Art and Beauty in the Middle Ages*. Translated by Hugh Bredin. New Haven: Yale University Press, 1986.
Farrer, Austin. *A Rebirth of Images: The Making of St. John's Apocalypse*. 1949. Reprinted, Eugene, OR: Wipf & Stock, 2006.
Foxe, John. *Foxe's Book of Martyrs*. Translated by G. A. Williamson. Boston: Little, Brown and Co., 1965.
Freud, Sigmund. *Moses and Monotheism*. Translated by Katherine Jones. New York: Knopf, 1939.
Garside, Charles. *Zwingli and the Arts*. New Haven: Yale University Press, 1966.
Gerrish, B. A. *Continuing the Reformation: Essays on Modern Religious Thought*. Chicago: University of Chicago Press, 1994.
Ghose, Sri Aurobindo. *The Supramental Manifestation*. London: Lotus, 1989.
Giakalis, Ambrosios. *Images of the Divine: The Theology of Icons at the Seventh Ecumenical Council*. Studies in the History of Christian Thought 54. Leiden: Brill, 1994.
Gilson, Etienne. *Christianity and Philosophy*. Translated by Ralph MacDonald. New York: Sheed & Ward, 1939.
Halbertal, Moshe, and Avishai Margalit. *Idolatry*. Translated by Naomi Goldblum. Cambridge: Harvard University Press, 1992.
Haller, William. *The Rise of Puritanism: Or, the Way to the New Jerusalem as Set Forth in Pulpit and Press from Thomas Cartwright to John Lilburne and John Milton, 1570–1643*. Philadelphia: University of Pennsylvania Press, 1972.
Harries, Karsten. *The Broken Frame: Three Lectures*. Washington, DC: Catholic University of America, 1989.
Hart, Hendrik, and Hohan van der Hoeven, and Nicholas Wolterstorff, editors. *Rationality in the Calvinian Tradition*. Christian Studies Today. Lanham, MD: University Press of America, 1983.
Hegel, G. W. F. *Encyclopaedia Logic*. Translated by T. F. Geraets, W. A. Suchting, and H. S. Harris. Indianapolis: Hackett, 1991.
———. *Hegel's Philosophy of Nature*. Translated by A. V. Miller. Oxford: Oxford University Press, 1970.
———. *Introduction to Aesthetics*. Translated by T. M. Knox. Oxford: Clarendon, 1979.

Bibliography

———. *Introduction to the Lectures on the History of Philosophy*. Translated by T. M. Knox and A. V. Miller. Oxford: Clarendon, 1985.

———. *Lectures on the History of Philosophy*. Translated by R. F. Brown and J. M. Stewart, with the assistance of H. S. Harris. Berkeley: University of California Press, 1990.

———. *Lectures on the Philosophy of Religion*. Translated by R. F. Brown, P. C. Hodson, and J. M. Stewart, with the assistance of H. S. Harris. Berkeley: University of California Press, 1984.

———. *Philosophy of Mind*. Translated by William Wallace and A. V. Miller. Oxford: Oxford University Press, 1971.

Henry, Patrick. "What Was the Iconoclastic Controversy About?" *Church History* 45 (1976) 25–41.

Hill, Christopher. *Change and Continuity in Seventeenth-Century England*. Rev. ed. New Haven: Yale University Press; 1991.

Hoopes, James. "Calvinism and Consciousness from Edwards to Beecher." In *Jonathan Edwards and the American Experience*. Edited by Nathan O. Hatch and Harry Stout. New York: Oxford University Press, 1988.

Huizinga, Johan. *The Waning of the Middle Ages: A Study of the Forms of Life, Thought, and Art in France and the Netherlands in the XIVth and XVth Centuries*. Translated by F. Hopman. Garden City, NY: Doubleday, 1954.

John of Damascus. *On the Divine Images: Three Apologies Against Those Who Attack the Divine Images*. Translated by David Anderson. 1980.

Kant, Immanuel. *The Critique of Judgement*. Translated by J. H. Bernard. New York: Hafner, 1951.

———. *Religion within the Limits of Reason Alone*. Translated by Theodore Green and Hoyt H. Hudson. New York: Harper & Row, 1960.

Keller, Catherine. "The Lost Fragrance: Protestantism and the Nature of What Matters." *Journal of the American Academy of Religion* 65 (1997) 355–70.

Kempis, Thomas. *The Imitation of Christ*. New York: Dover, 2003.

Kibbey, Ann. *The Interpretation of Material Shapes in Puritanism: A Study of Rhetoric, Prejudice, and Violence*. Cambridge Studies in American Literature and Culture 17. Cambridge: Cambridge University Press, 1986.

Kooi, Cornelis van der. "Within Proper Limits: Basic Features of John Calvin's Theological Epistemology." *Calvin Theological Journal* 29 (1994) 364–87.

Kuyper, Abraham. *Lectures on Calvinism*. Grand Rapids: Eerdmans, 1983.

Lawrence, D. H. "Why the Novel Matters." In *Modern Essays: Studying Language through Literature*, edited by R. C. Prasad. Bombay: Orient Longman Limited, 1987.

Leclercq, Jean. *The Love of Learning and the Desire for God*. Translated by Catherine Misrahi. New York: Fordham University Press, 1961.

Lee, Philip J. *Against the Protestant Gnostics*. Oxford: Oxford University Press, 1987.

Leith, John H. *John Calvin's Doctrine of the Christian Life*. Louisville: Westminster John Knox, 1989.

Lewis, C. S. *Letters to Malcolm: Chiefly on Prayer*. 1964. Reprinted, New York: Harvest Books, 1973.

———. *The Problem of Pain*. New York: Macmillian, 1962.

Limouris, Gennadios, compiler. *Icons, Windows on Eternity: Theology and Spirituality in Colour*. Faith and Order Paper 147. Geneva: WCC Publications, 1990.

Lovelace, Richard F. *Dynamics of Spiritual Life: An Evangelical Theology of Renewal*. Downers Grove, IL: InterVarsity, 1979.

Bibliography

Luther, Martin. *Against the Heavenly Prophets in the Matter of Images and Sacraments.* In *Luther's Works*, American edition, edited by Helmut T. Lehman and Jaroslav Pelikan, 40:79–223. Philadelphia: Fortress, 1955.

———. *Eight Sermons at Wittenberg.* In *Luther's Works*, 51:69–100.

———. "On the Bondage of the Will." In *Luther and Erasmus: Free Will and Salvation.* Edited by E. Gordon Rupp and Philip S. Watson. Philadelphia: Westminster, 1969.

Luxon, Thomas H. *Literal Figures: Puritan Allegory and the Reformation Crisis in Representation.* Chicago: University of Chicago Press, 1995.

Marsden, George. *Fundamentalism and American Culture: The Shaping of Twentieth-Century Evangelicalism: 1870–1925.* New York: Oxford University Press, 1980.

McConnell, Killian. *John Calvin, the Church and the Eucharist.* Princeton: Princeton University Press, 1967.

McDade, John. "The Evangelical Dimension of Catholicism." *The Month* 25 (1992) 257–66.

McGrath, Alister. *Evangelicalism and the Future of Christianity.* Downers Grove, IL: InterVarsity, 1995.

Merton, Robert. *Science, Technology and Society in Seventeenth Century England.* New York: Fertig, 1970.

Michalski, Sergiusz. *The Reformation and the Visual Arts: The Protestant Image Question in Western and Eastern Europe.* Christianity and Society in the Modern World. London: Routledge, 1993.

Miles, Margaret. *Augustine on the Body.* 1979. Reprinted, Eugene, OR: Wipf & Stock, 2010.

———. "Calvin on the Body." *Harvard Theological Review* 74 (1981) 303–23.

———. *Fullness of Life: Historical Foundations for a New Asceticism.* 1981. Reprinted, Eugene, OR: Wipf & Stock, 2006.

———. *Image as Insight: Visual Understanding in Western Christianity and Secular Culture.* 1985. Reprinted, Eugene, OR: Wipf & Stock, 2006.

Molnar, Thomas. *The Pagan Temptation.* Grand Rapids: Eerdmans, 1987.

Muller, Richard A. "Fides and Cognitio in Relation to the Problem of Intellect and Will in the Theology of John Calvin." *Calvin Theological Journal* 25 (1990) 207–24.

Murdoch, Iris. *The Fire and the Sun: Why Plato Banished the Poets.* Oxford: Oxford University Press, 1977.

Nietzsche, Friedrich. *The Birth of Tragedy.* Translated by Francis Golffing. New York: Doubleday, 1956.

———. *The Will to Power.* Translated by Walter Kaufmann and R. J. Hollingdale. New York: Random House, 1967.

Noll, Mark. *The Scandal of the Evangelical Mind.* Grand Rapids: Eerdmanns, 1994.

O'Meara, Thomas Franklin. "The Aesthetic Dimension in Theology." In *Art, Creativity, and the Sacred: An Anthology in Religion and Art*, edited by Diane Apostolos-Cappadona, 205–18. Rev. ed. New York: Crossroad, 1995.

Otto, Rudolf. *The Idea of the Holy.* 2nd ed. Translated by John W. Harvey. London: Oxford University Press, 1936.

Ozment, Steven. *The Age of Reform.* New Haven: Yale University Press, 1978.

———. *Protestantism: The Birth of a Revolution.* New York: Doubleday, 1992.

———. *The Reformation in the Cities: The Appeal of Protestantism to Sixteenth-Century Germany and Switzerland.* New Haven: Yale University Press, 1975.

Partee, Charles. *Calvin and Classical Philosophy.* Studies in the History of Christian Thought 14. Leiden: Brill, 1977.

Pelikan, Jaroslav. *The Christian Intellectual*. New York: Harper & Row, 1965.

———. *The Emergence of the Catholic Tradition, (100–600)*. The Christian Tradition 1. Chicago: University of Chicago Press, 1971.

———. *Imago Dei: The Byzantine Apologia For Icons*. Princeton: Princeton University Press, 1990.

———. *Obedient Rebels: Catholic Substance and Protestant Principle in Luther's Reformation*. New York: Harper & Row, 1964.

Pieper, Josef. *Scholasticism: Personalities and Problems of Medieval Philosophy*. Translated by Richard and Clara Winston. New York: McGraw-Hill, 1964.

Rice, Eugene F. Jr. *The Foundation of Early Modern Europe, 1460–1559*. New York: Norton, 1970.

Rice, Howard L. *Reformed Spirituality: An Introduction for Believers*. Ann Arbor, MI: Servant Books, 1991.

Roberts, Robert C. "Narrative Ethics." In *A Companion to Philosophy of Religion*. Edited by Philip L. Quinn and Charles Taliaferro. Blackwell Companions to Philosophy 9. Oxford: Blackwell, 1997.

Robinson, Edward. *Icons of the Present: Some Reflections on Art, the Sacred and the Holy*. London: SCM, 1993.

Scavizzi, Giuseppe. *The Controversy on Images: From Calvin to Baronius*. Toronto Studies in Religion 14. New York: Lang, 1992.

Scott, Robert A. *The Gothic Enterprise: A Guide to Understanding the Medieval Cathedral*. Berkeley, California: University of California Press, 2003.

Sider, Ronald J. *Andreas Bodenstein von Karlstadt: The Development of His Thought, 1517–1525*. Studies in Medieval and Reformation Thought 11. Leiden: Brill, 1974.

———. *Karlstadt's Battle with Luther: Documents in a Liberal-Radical Debate*. Philadelphia: Fortress, 1978.

Simpson, Alan. *Puritanism in Old and New England*. Chicago: University of Chicago Press, 1955.

Smith, John E. *Jonathan Edwards: Puritan, Preacher, Philosopher*. Notre Dame: University of Notre Dame Press, 1992.

Smith, Jonathan Z. *To Take Place: Toward Theory in Ritual*. Chicago Studies in the History of Judaism. Chicago: University of Chicago Press, 1987.

Southern, R.W. *Western Society and the Church in the Middle Ages*. New York: Penguin, 1970.

Steiner, George. *Real Presences*. Chicago: University of Chicago Press, 1989.

Stepelevich, Lawrence. "Hegel and Roman Catholicism." *Journal of the American Academy of Religion* 60 (1992) 673–91.

———. "Hegel and the Lutheran Eucharist." *Heythrop Journal* 27 (1991) 262–74.

Taylor, Charles. *Hegel*. New York: Cambridge University Press, 1975.

———. *Sources of the Self: The Making of Modern Identity*. Cambridge: Harvard University Press, 1987.

Troeltsch, Ernst. *Protestantism and Progress*. Translated by W. Montgomery. Boston: Beacon, 1966.

Ugolnik, Anthony. "The Libri Carolini: Antecedents of Reformation Iconoclasm." In *Iconoclasm and Drama*. Edited by Clifford Davidson and Ann Eljenholm Nichols. Western Michigan University, Medieval Institute Publications, 1989.

Underhill, Evelyn. *Worship*. 1923. Reprinted, Eugene, OR: Wipf & Stock, 2002.

Bibliography

Verdon, Timothy Gregory with John Dally, editors. *Monasticism and the Arts*. Syracuse: Syracuse University Press, 1984.

Walker, Williston. *A History of the Christian Church*. 3rd ed. New York: Scribner, 1970.

Warnock, Mary. "Imagination and Knowledge." *Theology* 32 (1988) 358–70.

Weber, Max. *The Protestant Ethic and the Spirit of Capitalism*. Translated by Talcott Parsons. London: Allen & Unwin, 1930.

———. *The Sociology of Religion*. Translated by Ephraim Fischoff. Boston: Beacon, 1963.

Westphal, Merold. "Hegel and the Reformation." In *Hegel, Freedom and Modernity*, 149–64. SUNY Series in Hegelian Studies. Albany: State University of New York Press, 1992.

White, Eugene E. *Puritan Rhetoric: The Issue of Emotion in Religion*. Landmarks in Rhetoric and Public Address. Carbondale: Southern Illinois University Press, 1972.

Whitehead, Alfred North. *Religion in the Making*. 1926. Reprinted, Cambridge: Cambridge University Press, 2011.

———. *Modes of Thought*. New York: Capricorn, 1938.

———. *Symbolism: Its Meaning and Effect*. New York: Macmillan, 1927.

Willey, Basil. *The Seventeenth-Century Background: Studies in the Thought of the Age in Relation to Poetry and Religion*. Garden City, NY: Doubleday Anchor Books, 1953.

Willis-Watkins. "Reform by Eliminating the Use of Images." *Studies in Reformed Theology and History* 2 (1994) 22–59.

www.ingramcontent.com/pod-product-compliance
Lightning Source LLC
Chambersburg PA
CBHW050820160426
43192CB00010B/1829